THE DELL
ENCYCLOPEDIA OF
DOGS

A. Singer

The Dell Encyclopedia of

DOGS

by Lou Sawyer Ashworth
Medical Entries by Irene Kraft,
MRCVS, DVM

Illustrated by Arthur Singer,
Walter Wright and Ann Brewster

Delacorte Press / New York

Published by
Delacorte Press

An original work created and produced by
Vineyard Books, Inc.
159 East 64 Street
New York, New York 10021

ISBN 0-440-01784-X DELACORTE PRESS
Printed in Italy by Arnoldo Mondadori Editore, Sp A

Introduction

This handbook attempts to answer in concise form most of the questions that might be asked by a dog owner or prospective owner. Readers interested in more extensive treatment of the entries are referred to the Bibliography on page 239, which lists some of the many admirable volumes available to those interested in the history and development of the dog.

Within these pages will be found virtually all breeds currently recognized throughout the world, together with brief descriptions of their conformation, special aptitudes and temperament; a listing of most of the ailments to which dogs are subject, together with their symptoms and prognosis; historical notes and anatomical details, plus more extended entries on behavior patterns, care, housing and training.

Special thanks go to Mary Gay Sargent who spent many weeks reading and editing the entries; to Teddy Longo and Topper, her superb Poodle who posed for the obedience training sequences; and to Nancy Parker whose wonderful Norwich Terrier, Tuffy, patiently ran through her repertoire of tricks again and again. We are grateful also to Herbert O. Wegner, Robert C. Ballard and Irina Martino who contributed aid and guidance on such widely varied subject matters as scent hurdle racing, Karabash dogs and Schutzhund training; to Ivan Kovacs for information on the Canaan Dog; and, among many others, to Billie Kern, Judy Bard, Barbara McCrudden, Phyllis Roitsch, Vija Lapins, and Sue Wilson. Finally, our thanks go to Janis Leventhal, who helped enormously in nursing the entire project through from A to Z.

The Egyptian god Anubis was part dog, part jackal.

A NOTE ABOUT THE ENTRIES:

Breeds are generally listed under the designation most frequently employed. Thus, the *Japanese Akita* will be found under *Akita* and *Welsh Corgis* under *Cardigan Welsh Corgi* and *Pembroke Welsh Corgi*. When the national label is most frequently used—for example, *Norwegian Buhund*—descriptions will be found under that heading.

The classification of breeds and some of the areas in which they are officially recognized for show purposes will be found at the conclusion of an entry under the following numerical code:

1–Recognized by the American Kennel Club.

2–Recognized by the English Kennel Club.

3–Recognized by the Canadian Kennel Club.

4–Recognized by the Australian National Kennel Council.

M–is used to denote Miscellaneous, a non-classification employed only in the United States.

This book does not attempt to give precise standards for each breed, since a score or more factors come into play in determining the perfection of an individual animal. Weights and heights of individual breeds are included and generally conform to breed standards. They are, however, included primarily to give the prospective owner of a dog a general idea of the physical attributes of the breed. In almost all breeds it can be assumed that the weight and height of a bitch is less than that of a male animal.

A

ABDOMEN: Enlargement of a dog's abdominal area or tenderness to the touch may be a symptom of any one of many problems, ranging from simple gastritis to an abnormal growth. If the condition does not subside in a day or so, a veterinarian should be consulted.

ABERDEEN TERRIER: see *Scottish Terrier*.

ABORTION: premature delivery of immature young—usually before they are sufficiently developed to sustain life. Injuries, illness, shock, hereditary influences, or unknown factors may cause a pregnant bitch to abort.

A bitch who miscarries should be taken, with her dead puppies, to a veterinarian as soon as possible, so a possible diagnosis can be made. Ill or not, a dog who aborts a number of times should no longer be bred.

ABSCESS: a collection of pus formed by the disintegration of tissue. It can occur in any area of the body but in dogs is most common under the skin. Abscesses are usually the result of puncture wounds from a dog bite. The pus will eventually rupture through the skin and cause ugly wounds; therefore it is best to have the abscess drained surgically by a veterinarian. Loss of coat around the abscess almost always occurs but, in all but severe cases, it grows back quickly when the wound heals.

ACCESS: A means to reach fenced-in areas can be provided by a pet doorway with plastic shutters which are self-closing after the dog goes out or returns. These pet doorways come in all sizes and can be easily fitted into walls, doors, garages or doghouses, permitting the pet to leave or return at will and putting an end to scratched surfaces.

It's simple to install a dog door.

ACID MILK: caused by an illness in a nursing bitch. Puppies do not thrive when extreme acidity is present in the mother's milk but a veterinarian can usually correct the condition or put the puppies on a formula until the bitch is cured.

Affenpinscher

AFFENPINSCHER: This charming and comical little "monkey terrier" (*affe* is the German word for "monkey") has two better-known descendants—the Miniature Schnauzer and the Brussels Griffon. It was developed in Germany more than a century ago, but began to grow in popularity elsewhere after World War II. Black is the preferred color for its coarse, wiry coat, but it will lose no points at dog shows if black is mixed with tan, red, or gray. The breed is small but somewhat on the noisy side. Weight ranges from 7 to 8 pounds, and the dog should stand no more than 10 inches high at the shoulder. (Toy: 1–2)

AFFIX: in the U.K., the kennel name of the breeder.

AFGHAN HOUND: Dating back several thousand years, this aris-tocrat of dogdom developed its long, silky coat in Afghanistan. The Afghan is a sight hound, whose keen vision enables it to spot game at far distances while its swivel-hipped body and blazing speed enable it to pursue a zigzag course in overtaking prey. Although in theory the Afghan should be given a vast amount of territory to exercise in, this elegant and regal animal has become increasingly popular as a house pet. It is affectionate and well behaved, although on occasions it may prove shy and a bit uneasy in the presence of strangers. Dogs are 27 inches in height, weighing around 60 pounds; bitches, 25 inches and 50 pounds. (Hound: 1–2–3–4)

Afghan Hound

AFTERBIRTH: see *whelping*.

AGE: see *life span*.

AGED DOGS: Like people, more dogs live a lot longer than they did fifty years ago. Also, they suffer the same kind of old-age indig-nities—cataracts, deafness, heart and kidney diseases, diabetes, tooth and gum troubles, over-weight, and tumors. If your dog begins to slow down, seek the advice of a veterinarian. Peculiarities of the breed, combined with the medical history of the individual dog, will help him to decide if dietetic changes are in order. Unless your dog is actively ill, nurse it at home. A friendly word spoken by a familiar voice is often the best medicine of all.

Akita

Airedale Terrier

AIREDALE TERRIER: Largest of the terriers, the Airedale is an all-around performer—as a guard and as a guide for the blind, as a hunter and as a water dog. It is dependable, extremely good-looking, and a devoted companion. Named after the town in Yorkshire where the dog was first shown nearly a century ago, the Airedale lost some of its popularity in recent decades but now appears to be on the way up. Dogs are 23 inches at the shoulders and approximately 43 pounds; bitches a bit less. (Terrier: 1–2–3–4)

A.K.C.: American Kennel Club.

AKITA: a native of the Japanese island of Honshu, this very large dog (25½ to 27½ inches tall, weight from 75 to 110 pounds) looks much like the Chow Chow, except that it has short to medium-length hair and lacks the blue mouth and tongue of its Chinese cousin. The breed is used for hunting and guard duties in its homeland. Highly teachable, these dogs were first brought to the United States by occupation soldiers after World War II who saw their potential as working dogs. Any color is permissible, though white should total no more than a third overall. (M:1; Utility: 2)

ALASKAN MALAMUTE: Some idea of the endurance of this admirable sled dog is indicated by the performance of a lead dog for a team that pulled half a ton of freight more than a thousand miles over an Alaskan mountain trail in mid-winter and a month later covered 408 miles in a bit more than seventy-two hours. The name came from the Mahlemut tribe of western Alaska, whom the big, rugged dogs served faithfully as workers and family favorites. The Malamutes easily adapt to all climates and all conditions, making them tolerant and gentle companions. Males range from 23 inches

Alaskan Malamute

to 25 inches at the shoulder and weigh from 75 to 85 pounds; bitches are a bit less. Coat colors range from light gray to black, with white on the underbody, feet and legs, and facial mask. (Working: 1–2–3)

ALBINO: without pigmentation.

ALENTEJO HERDER: an ancient Portuguese working dog (25 to 29 inches at the withers) with a bear-like head, short coarse coat, and a well-deserved reputation for nocturnal alertness and cattle herding ability.

Alentejo Herder

ALLERGIES, *DOG:* There is every evidence that dogs are just as subject to allergies as people are. Foods or drugs or plant pollens produce sneezing, coughing, itching, skin rashes, or diarrhea in dogs sensitive to one or more of these agents. A veterinarian may conduct skin or food tests if he suspects an allergy. One can help by outlining to him the onset of symptoms. Treatment is possible in some cases where the allergy-producing substance cannot be eliminated from the dog's normal environment.

ALLERGIES, *HUMAN:* "Every boy should have a dog" does not apply to the boy (or girl, or man, or woman) who has recognized allergies. Hay fever and asthma should be included in this category. No matter how the dog is brushed, hair may aggravate an existing human allergic pattern. Poodles and Kerry Blues are among the few dogs that shed very little, but even they cause trouble for victims of chronic asthma. Check with a physician before acquiring a dog if subject to allergies.

ALOPECIA: see *shedding*.

ALPINE MASTIFF: see *Saint Bernard*.

ALSATIAN: see *German Shepherd*.

ALTER: see *castration*.

AMERICAN COCKER SPANIEL: A separate breed from the English Cocker Spaniel, this popular and sprightly dog is somewhat smaller than its British relative. Its skull is more prominent, it has a shorter muzzle and a long, heavy coat. The sturdy little American Cocker is rarely used for hunting these days (although it is most proficient at it), but is more often seen in the show ring and in the role of a devoted house companion. Size ranges from 14 to 15 inches in

American Cocker

height and from 22 to 28 pounds in weight. Coat colors can be solid black, solid color other than black, black and tan, or parti-color. (Sporting: 1–3; Gundog: 2–4)

AMERICAN COONHOUND: see *Black-and-Tan Coonhound*.

AMERICAN FIELD: Nearly 100 years ago, the *American Field* began to publish a magazine and hold its first formal field trials for pointing dogs. Since 1900 it has issued the *Field Dog Stud Book*, as well as governed field trials following rules set up by the Amateur Field Trial Clubs of America. It registers nearly 30,000 hunting dogs a year, chiefly Pointers and English Setters. *The American Field Magazine* publishes results of all the 750-odd trials a year held by its affiliated clubs, as well as some run under American Kennel Club regulations.

AMERICAN FOXHOUND: Ancestors of this breed are said to have come to American shores in 1650. Early-day aristocrats like George Washington favored the dogs, in later years Irish imports were brought in. Today's foxhunter uses the breed in the Unites States in four ways: (1) as a field-trial hound; (2) for hunting with a gun;

(3) as a trail or drag hound; (4) as a pack hound. Different characteristics are required for each sport, and the animals are bred accordingly. Whatever their function, these 21- to 25-inch-high dogs are born and bred to the hunt. (Hound: 1–2–3–4)

American Foxhound

AMERICAN KENNEL CLUB: official registrar of purebred dogs in the United States and the largest organization of its type in the world. Known by its initials, AKC, the studbook it keeps added 1.1 million entries in 1972 covering 118 recognized breeds. Poodles headed the list with 218,899 registrations, Field Spaniels wound it up with just three. The AKC also annually licenses upward of 1,000 championship shows and an almost equal number of field trials, as well as nearly 700 obedience trials. In addition, the AKC licenses and supervises the activities of some 2,300 show judges and nearly 800 professional handlers.

The organization publishes many books and pamphlets on training and breed standards as well as the magazine, *Pure Bred Dogs-American Kennel Gazette*.

The Club's roster of registrations

11

for 1972 showed that the 20 most popular breeds in the United States were:

1. Poodles
2. German Shepherds
3. Beagles
4. Dachshunds
5. Irish Setters
6. Miniature Schnauzers
7. St. Bernards
8. Labrador Retrievers
9. Collies
10. Doberman Pinschers
11. American Cocker Spaniels
12. Pekingese
13. Chihuahuas
14. Shetland Sheepdogs
15. Basset Hounds
16. Great Danes
17. Yorkshire Terriers
18. Pomeranians
19. Brittany Spaniels
20. Golden Retrievers

Poodles continue to lead the American popularity parade.

The beautiful Irish Setter is fast growing in favor.

The happy little Beagle is the top hound in the U.S.A.

The Collie has retained his popularity for decades.

Labradors have long held the number one position among Retrievers.

German Shepherds have enjoyed great favor since the days of Rin Tin Tin.

Dachshunds—high on the list and still moving up.

The massive St. Bernard, rarely a worker these days, is a favored house pet.

Dobermans have risen fast on the hit parade.

The Miniature Schnauzer is tremendously popular today as a house pet and watch dog.

AMERICAN SOCIETY FOR THE PREVENTION OF CRUELTY TO ANIMALS (ASPCA): a designation applied only to the organization founded in New York in 1874, though the concept that both work animals and pets deserve humane treatment quickly spread through the United States. In 1877, a national group called the American Humane Society was formed, and other societies soon came into existence. Whatever they are called, these groups are composed of local residents who concern themselves with proper care of animals, public-education programs, improved laboratory conditions for animals, in some cases antivivisection programs, and the establishment of shelters that accept unwanted animals and round up homeless dogs and cats.

AMERICAN STAFFORDSHIRE TERRIER: see *Staffordshire Terrier*.

AMERICAN WATER SPANIEL: Smaller than its relative, the Irish Water Spaniel, and minus the distinguishing rat tail, this is one of a handful of breeds native to the United States. Related perhaps to the Poodle and extinct English Water Spaniel, this dog was developed chiefly to hung inland water

American Water Spaniel.

17

water birds along the Mississippi River flyway and its tributaries and where lakes and ponds are within walking distance of each other. The dog's relatively small size (15 to 18 inches at the shoulder) and good color, which blends with woods and fields in Autumn, make it ideal for moving in close to game birds. Weight: dogs 28 to 45 pounds; bitches a bit less. (Sporting: 1–3)

ANAL IRRITATION: most often caused by excess fluid in the anal sacs which are located on each side of the rectum, about one-fourth of an inch from the exterior. An anal gland infection may be indicated when the dog drags its rear along the ground. A veterinarian will treat the condition by expressing the foul-smelling secretion from the anal sacs and packing the infected area with antibiotics.

ANATOLIAN KARABASH: This handsome and rugged Turkish sheep dog has served double duty in its native land—as herd dog and agricultural guard by day; protecting live stock and crops from wild boars and other marauders at night. *Karabash* means blackhead

Anatolian Karabash

and describes their traditional muzzle and ear coloration. The breed is somewhat suspicious of strangers, highly protective where the owner's land or possessions are concerned, gentle with children and makes a good pet. For a big dog (45 pounds and up, 22 inches in height) the Karabash is generally a light eater. The breed was recognized in England in 1965 but is almost unknown in the United States. (Working: 2)

ANATOMY, EXTERNAL,: see illustration on pages 20 and 21.

ANATOMY, INTERNAL AND SKELETAL: see illlustrations on pages 22 and 23.

ANCESTORS: see *evolution*.

ANEMIA: may be caused by improper diet resulting in a vitamin deficiency or a wide variety of other factors. Symptoms: the inside surface of the gums, eyelids, and other mucous membranes are pale and the dog may tire easily or breathe at a fast rate. A veterinarian should be consulted for treatment.

ANESTHESIA: means without feeling. Anesthetics are drugs used to eliminate the pain of surgical procedures, and may be (1) local and involve only a small area; for example, prior to the removal of a localized tumor; or (2) general; causing unconsciousness. A veterinarian induces them into the blood by intravenous injection, or through the lungs by the inhalation of various mixtures of special gases. Unless an emergency operation is performed, the dog should not be fed for at least 12 hours before surgery requiring general anesthesia.

ANGULATION: Angles formed by a meeting of the bones, especially the shoulder to upper arm, and stifle to hock.

A.N.K.C.: Australian National Kennel Council.

ANTISEPTIC: a substance that slows the growth of bacteria, without killing them, and without destroying or injuring live tissues. Mild soap and hydrogen peroxide are the only antiseptics that can be used safely by pet owners inexperienced in medical practice.

Veterinarians use a wide variety of antiseptics in treating wounds, infections, and for surgical purposes. (See also *disinfectants*.)

ARGENTINE: The National authority is the Kennel Club Argentino, Florida 671, Buenos Aires.

ARTERY: the main vessel that carries blood from the heart to all parts of the body. If a dog is injured, one can tell immediately whether it has suffered a cut artery (which is serious and requires immediate attention), since blood spurts from the wound in a pulsating rhythm.

ARTHRITIS: inflammation of a joint.

ARTIFICIAL INSEMINATION: the collection of semen from a male in an artificial vagina and then its transfer by syringe to the cervix of a bitch in heat. This is done when natural mating cannot or should not be accomplished, and can increase the productivity of a desirable stud, since semen can be frozen for later use or can accomplish mating between dogs geographically separated. Much research is currently being done in this field.

In Great Britain, if one gets prior permission for registration of the expected litter from the Kennel Club, the puppies can be registered exactly as if they were the progeny of a natural mating. Application for such registration must be accompanied by a veterinarian's statement that the artificial process is necessary or justified. In the United States the AKC accepts registrations of such litters only if both the dam and the sire are present during the process, and if both extraction and insemination are done by the same vet. Owners of both dogs must sign the breeding certificate.

ARTIFICIAL RESPIRATION: given by placing the dog on the breastbone, tongue out, while pushing the ribs in with the flat of the hand.

ASTHMA: a condition in which the bronchi and bronchioles (small bronchi) constrict and produce excess mucus so that the dog is unable to get sufficient air into its lungs. Symptoms include difficulty in breathing with the mouth open and front legs held widely apart. True asthma is rare in dogs. It is considered to be a form of allergy caused by dust or chemical irritants in the air, but can also occur as a complication of heart disease. Treatment must be begun promptly in acute cases to prevent death by asphyxiation.

AUSTRALIAN CATTLE DOG: These dogs work at rounding up, driving, and herding range cattle into pens in their native Australia. Since this is the sole job of the breed, they have been developed over a period of more than a cen-

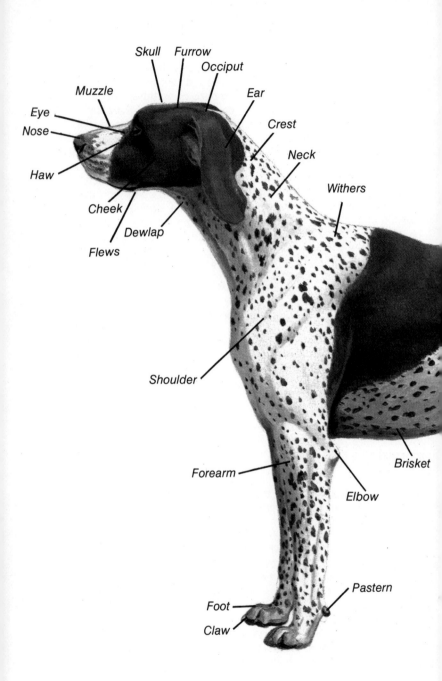

Skull Furrow

Occiput

Muzzle

Ear

Eye

Crest

Nose

Neck

Haw

Withers

Cheek

Dewlap

Flews

Shoulder

Forearm

Brisket

Elbow

Pastern

Foot

Claw

EXTERNAL ANATOMY

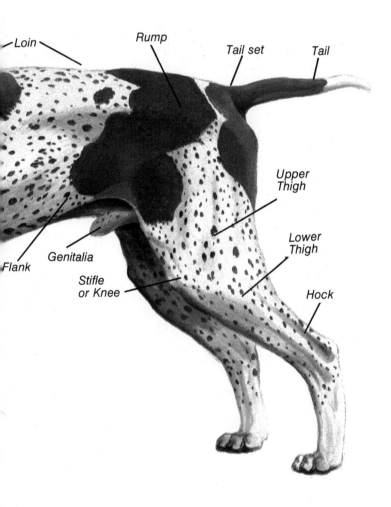

Loin

Rump

Tail set

Tail

Flank

Genitalia

Stifle
or Knee

Upper
Thigh

Lower
Thigh

Hock

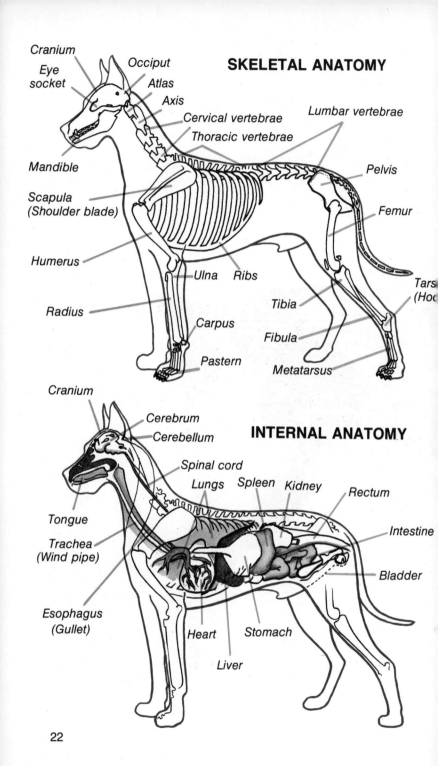

SKELETAL ANATOMY

Cranium
Occiput
Eye socket
Atlas
Axis
Cervical vertebrae
Thoracic vertebrae
Lumbar vertebrae
Mandible
Pelvis
Scapula (Shoulder blade)
Femur
Humerus
Ulna
Ribs
Tars (Hoc
Radius
Tibia
Fibula
Carpus
Pastern
Metatarsus

INTERNAL ANATOMY

Cranium
Cerebrum
Cerebellum
Spinal cord
Lungs
Spleen
Kidney
Rectum
Tongue
Intestine
Trachea (Wind pipe)
Bladder
Esophagus (Gullet)
Heart
Stomach
Liver

22

Australian Cattle Dog

tury to be smart, fast, tireless, and sharp biters. (It takes more than a gentle nip at an angry steer's hind leg to get him to move.)

One of the miscellaneous breeds recognized by the AKC, few of these dogs are shown in the United States. Mature dogs average about 18 inches at the shoulder and weigh from 34 to 40 pounds. (M:1; Working:4)

AUSTRALIAN KELPIE: Another of Australia's working dogs, the Kelpie specializes in working with sheep. Often out of sight of the herder, the dog follows a flock and keeps it together, moves up front to settle leadership quarrels, and can cut out a portion of the flock and lead it to a water hole while it makes the balance wait its turn. The breed traces its ancestry to Scottish sheep dogs exported to Australia long ago.

Australian Kelpie

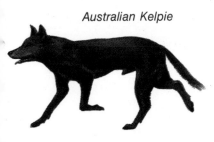

A grown dog is 18 to 20 inches tall; bitches are somewhat smaller. The short coat can be black, black and tan, chocolate, smoke blue, fawn, red, or red and tan. Ears are prick. The body should be a fraction longer than the dog's height. (M:1; Working: 2–3–4)

AUSTRALIAN NATIONAL KENNEL COUNCIL: As of this time the ANKC recognizes 107 breeds that may compete at Championship Shows for the title "Aust. Ch." Each of Australia's States and Territories has its own canine organization—New South Wales, Queensland, South Australia, Tasmania, Victoria, Western Australia, Australian Capital Territory, and Northern Territory—but the ANKC is the advisory body to all of them. Formed in 1958, it does not stage dog shows, but through its member body, the Kennel Control Council, reciprocal arrangements exist with all States of the Commonwealth. The Melbourne Royal Show, a key event, is held under the Control Council's rules. Address: Royal Show Grounds, Ascot Vale, Victoria, Australia, 3032.

AUSTRALIAN TERRIER: "Compact" is the word for this small dog, which can point to not one but at least five kinds of British terriers as its forebears. The breed became popular in Australia before the turn of the century for its speed and agility in hunting rats, rabbits, and snakes. It began to achieve modest popularity in Great Britain in the 1920's and was recognized in the United States in 1960.

Most representatives of the breed in the United States weigh

23

Australian Terrier

genverband, Karl-Schweighofer-Gasse, 3, A-1070, Vienna.

AUTOMOBILE CHASING: Some dogs become inveterate chasers of vehicles. The only known cure is to induce in the animal a desire to abstain through a traumatic experience. Possible solution: enlist friends to drive a car past the spot where the dog begins his usual pursuit. As he ranges alongside: (a) dump a pail of water with ammonia added on him, or (b) discharge the contents of a water gun containing water and fortified by ammonia in his face, or (c) throw a length of chain in his direction. None of these are guaranteed to produce the desired effect but, however draconian they may seem, any one of the three is preferable to a dead dog or a wrecked car.

from 12 to 14 pounds; in England they are somewhat lighter. The coat can be either blue-black or silver-black and can have deep tan, sand-color, or clear red markings on the head and legs. (Terrier: 1–2–3–4)

AUSTRIA: The national ruling body is *Osterreichischer Kynolo-*

B

BAD BREATH: has many causes and a veterinarian is best equipped to make a diagnosis and to recommend treatment. Excess tartar on teeth, sinus conditions, ulcers of mouth or gums are some of the causes. Products that claim to neutralize the odor may make your animal more pleasant to live with, but won't cure it.

BAD MANNERS: are most easily avoided in dogs by sensible handling of the puppy, from the time of its arrival in the home. Puppies can be taught good manners with gentle, patient, and consistent corrections. More formal training can be acquired later in obedience classes which are proliferating all over the world. In addition, many books and pamphlets on training are published. (See also *obedience training*.)

BALANCED: symmetrical in proportions.

BANDAGING: Most minor cuts and wounds should be left open so that the dog may lick the injured area. Bandaging is essential, however, to control bleeding from severe cuts and injuries to a dog's pads. Apply a sterile dressing to the wound, cover with a pad of cotton (cotton wool) and bandage as tightly as possibly with gauze wrapping. For further protection of the bandage, which should be left on for several days, cover with strips of adhesive tape.

Head and ear bandages can be protected with a tubular structure—a sock or sleeve from a knitted garment. These are fitted, cap-style, over the head and anchored with adhesive tape. Body wounds can also be partially protected from a dog's attempts to remove the bandage by covering it with an ordinary dog sweater or coat. (See also *Elizabethan collar, tourniquet*.)

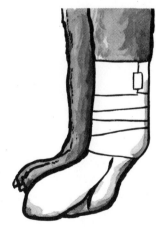

A cut pad should be bandaged.

BARREL: the ribs and body.

BARREL-LEGGED: when the front legs are bowed.

BASENJI: This agile little dog who doesn't bark (but does growl, whine and yodel) is of African origin and almost certainly was a house pet in ancient Egypt. It is meticulous in its habits, washing itself in cat fashion. A unique breed, some Basenjis show little inclination to form close attachments to human beings and many bitches still maintain a once-a-year heat cycle—two typical characteristics of undomesticated animals.

Although in many respects not a true hound, the Basenji can be trained to retrieve game, track injured animals, and point. Mature dogs are from 16 to 17 inches tall, and weigh 22 to 24 pounds. For show purposes they can be all black, all red, or black and tan. Breed standards allow white feet or legs, chest, or collar on the black-and-tans. (Hound: 1–2–3–4)

Bassett Griffon Vendeen

begun to achieve recognition abroad. In France it is the most numerous of all hounds. Its rough, harsh coat, straight legs, alert bearing, and "let's go" manner make it more terrier- than hound-like in its hunting habits. The Vendeen is divided into three catagories—Briquet, Grand, and Petit, and ranges in size from nearly 20 inches down to less than 15 inches in height. (Hound: 2)

Basset Hound

BASSET HOUND: Bred centuries ago in France solely for the hunt, the Basset makes up in tenacity, courage, and keeness of scent what it lacks in speed—and to watch these solid citizens go galumphing across an open field is a joy unto itself. More and more Bassets are being converted into house pets these days, and, although they are highly amiable and more than willing to please,

Basenji

BASSET GRIFFON VENDEEN: a native of the Vendee Department of western France, this medium-sized hound has only recently

they are by nature outdoor dogs. Not the easiest dog to train, it is rarely seen in the obedience ring, and when a Basset gives tongue —a sound that sportsmen claim is the most beautiful of all hound-music—it is possible that nonhunting neighbors may dissent. Height: 14 inches in the United States; slightly taller dogs are acceptable in Great Britain. Weight: around 50 pounds. (Hound: 1–2–3–4)

Bat ears

BAT EARS: upstanding ears, rounded at the top, broad at the base, and facing forward.

BATHS: Since dogs don't sweat, and since brushing and combing usually keeps their coats clean and odor-free, most breeds need to be bathed at infrequent intervals. If a dog rolls in axle grease, mistakes a skunk for a friend, or needs a prescribed medicated bath, here's how: Put it into a bathtub or an old-fashioned laundry tub (deep sink or washtub if it is a small dog). Lightly plug its ears with absorbent cotton. Put a drop or two of mineral oil in each eye. Wet the coat thoroughly. Using a mild soap or shampoo, start from the head (keeping the soap out of its eyes) and work lather back and then down the legs to the feet. Rinse with clear water, using, if you have one, a spray hose of the type beauty shops use. Wrap a big beach towel around the dog when it begins to shake itself dry. A vigorous toweling afterward will be all that's necessary. Keep the dog inside for an hour or two if it is cold outdoors.

BAY: a hunting hound's voice.

BEAGLE: This happy little fellow is enormously in favor wherever rabbits or hare are hunted. In the United States, where Beagling is an extremely popular sport, it rates among the top five in registrations. It performs beautifully in field trials and in the show ring, but is less frequently outstanding in obedience trials. Like its relative, the Basset, it is on the stubborn side, and not overeasy to train. It is also well to mention that a Beagle who spots a rabbit in the backyard or in a nearby patch of woods will give voice. Its mournful howls, however, do not denote unhappiness, but rather joy and the challenge of competition. Today, Beagles are generally bred in two sizes: the smaller should not exceed 13 inches at the withers; a somewhat larger version should be more than 13 inches but not above 15. Its

Beagle

color may be any of the typical "hound" colors; usually white with a variation of tan or tan and black markings. (Hound: 1−2−3−4)

Bearded Collie

BEARDED COLLIE: a working dog, used for driving sheep and cattle, chiefly in Scotland, though it appears to have emigrated from Poland several centuries ago. Unlike rough and smooth Collies, the breed has ears that hang close to the head. A medium-sized animal, 20 to 22 inches tall, it has a long, lean body and a moderately long double coat. Breeders aren't particular about color. (Working: 2)

BEAUCERON: This French shepherd dog, like the Doberman Pinscher which it resembles, is usually black and tan or black with considerable variations—for example, gray with black markings. A good worker, it was until recently

Beauceron

classified as a rare breed, but it is now officially recognized in Great Britain. (Working: 2)

BEDDING AND BEDS: Kennel owners often use wood shavings or straw to keep their dogs comfortable. House dogs are happy with old towels, washable blankets, or foam-rubber cushions covered with washable material. Some dogs prefer a box or dog bed; inevitably, some consider their owner's bed the best bet.

Puppies who have been weaned need disposable bedding—newspapers in a carton or box—which can be changed daily until they are old enough not to soil their quarters at night.

If your house is drafty at floor level, build or buy a bed, enclosed on three sides, which is elevated a little off the floor. Wicker baskets, wooden boxes, wire crates, or fiberglass structures with aluminum bonded to the edges are all satisfactory as permanent quarters. Puppies chew their beds, as well as everything else within reach, until they are through teething, so don't invest in a bed of chewable material until the pup is six months old or more.

BEDLINGTON TERRIER: In the eighteenth century in its native England the breed once had short legs and a sturdy body and was invaluable for catching rats. Crossbreeding (perhaps with Whippets) produced a dog lamb-like in appearance with the speed of a hound, long legs, and a knack for rabbit hunting. Today the Bedlington is a house dog and rarely hunts. The breed, which stands from 15½ to 16½ inches high and

Bedlington Terrier

weighs between 17 and 23 pounds, is gentle and well-mannered. Coats must be scissor-trimmed, but once you've seen it done, it is not difficult to master the art. Blue and liver are the most frequently seen colors, but mixtures with sandy tones and tan are acceptable. (Terrier: 1–2–3–4)

BED SORES: result from sleeping on hard floors, or because old or sick dogs are unable to change positions often enough to shift their weight away from bony or vulnerable joints. Softer bedding will help.

BEE and WASP STINGS: If possible, remove stingers, then apply a paste of baking soda and water.

BEHAVIOR PATTERNS:

ADULT (normal): Where "instincts" leave off and "behavior patterns" begin is a highly complex subject. Puppies instinctively find their way to the dam's teats to nurse and crawl away from their beds to urinate or defecate. Adult dogs often turn in a tight circle two or three times before lying down. Dogs hunt by sight, by scenting on the ground, or by picking up scents from the wind. Which method used seems to depend on inherited instincts, yet these instincts can be successfully modified by training to combine two or more methods. They fight in the same way the ancestors of their breed did, even if they have never fought before.

Some experts maintain that "guardian instincts," particularly developed in many of the working breeds, is less a matter of inheritance than a willingness to adapt to training, but this position is hotly contested by those who point out that many untrained dogs show an early instinctive tendency to guard the owner, his children or his possessions.

Present knowledge indicates that *all* breeds of dogs have equal intelligence, with individuals in many breeds demonstrating exceptionally high mental capacity. The longer a dog's attention span, the easier it is to train. Some individuals can't focus on anything for more than a few fleeting seconds, and are thus incapable of

From puppyhood onward most Retrievers instinctively take to the water.

At two weeks these nursing Cocker pups are still defenseless.

"learning," though they may be able to solve their own problems handily. Others "concentrate" and learn quickly and almost effortlessly. Some breeds are typically easier to train than others, perhaps because they can concentrate long enough to associate rewards with the prompt execution of commands.

On one point all experts are in agreement—that the experiences during the puppy weeks (three through 10 weeks) have a crucial effect on the behavior patterns of the adult animal.

A mother's care plus the companionship of litter mates and human beings are key factors that affect a dog's later life.

ADULT (abnormal): These can be classified for general purposes as follows:

1. Disease
2. Frustration and boredom
3. Old age
4. Shock or trauma
5. Homosexuality
6. Spite
7. Fear-biting (see *shyness*)
8. Pack instincts
9. Cannibalism among bitches with new litters, the causes of which are unknown.

Physical disturbances can cause depraved appetite. Glandular upsets, poor diet, or hookworms may cause a dog to eat feces. A tumor in the testicle may cause a male dog to attract other males as a bitch in heat would.

Chained or caged dogs bark and lunge to get attention. Failure to get it may cause them to turn to biting or eating stones and other foreign objects.

Old dogs often become irritable and incontinent. Failing eyesight, deafness, and kidney troubles are likely contributing factors.

Severe emotional shocks tend to produce biting or emptying of stomach, intestines, or bladder if the circumstances that produced the original fright are repeated.

Homosexuality among dogs who have been brought up together is fairly routine, but it is rare that such dogs, as adults, will fail to mate normally.

Spoiled dogs, like spoiled children, will lash out at their owners if they are not given their own way, particularly if left alone. They may bark or howl for endless hours or defecate on their owner's bed.

Dogs who are individually gentle may, if they fall in with a pack, attack people and other animals. Don't let your dog roam unsupervised.

PUPPIES: Puppies are born virtually defenseless. They can't see, hear or stand up. They can nurse, cry, and demonstrate reflex muscular action. Not until they are about three to four weeks old can they begin to see well and react to sounds. At twenty-one to twenty-four days they growl, chew on a brother's or sister's ear, wag their tails, engage in play-behavior, and begin to satisfy their curiosity about everything in reach. Between the twenty-first and thirty-

Three Lhasa Apso pups await a chance to socialize.

Dachshunds discovering the facts of life

fifth days of life, it is crucial for a puppy to socialize with people (as well as with its litter mates). The relationship between man and dog, once established, will last for the dog's lifetime, through good times and bad.

No puppy should be taken away from its dam and its litter mates until it is weaned (at forty-two to forty-nine days of age). A dog deprived of this necessary companionship may become a psychological misfit, bewildered about who it is, belligerent toward other dogs, unable to adapt to new surroundings, and unfriendly to people who are not its owners.

Phase two in a puppy's life begins when it is about five weeks old. If it has been raised in a kennel run or cage, it should be brought for brief periods into the home either of the breeder or of the person who will be its new owner so that it won't be afraid of new surroundings or overprotective about its own territory. (See *territorial rights*). As soon as possible it should be walked around the

A Pembroke Welsh Corgi puppy thinks things over.

neighborhood on a leash and taken for short rides in a car, if the family has one. At about this time a puppy can be taught to obey simple commands—to come when called, for example.

Puppies get interested in sex at about four weeks of age, and begin to mount their siblings, regardless of sex. A male dog will start to raise

Yorkshire and Boston Terrier pups (above) and a basket full of Boxer pups (below) in varying moods of expectancy.

Probing to find what lies beyond the fringe.

his leg to urinate sometime after five months of age. Females usually squat. Urine is the canine postal-telephone service. It tells the next dog that comes by who's been in the neighborhood, where it's going, how its health is, whether it has been eating regularly, whether it is in heat and looking for a mate. Occasionally a dog will urinate on the spot where it has just buried a bone, to remind itself where the bone is the next time it passes by.

While its behavior may periodically irritate or anger its owner, almost anything a puppy does is considered normal if it is healthy and sociable. If you have a short temper and pride in your possessions, keep shoes, gloves, socks, and other tempting items out of the puppy's reach.

BELGIAN GROENENDAEL: This sheepdog's talents for herding are no longer greatly in demand. However, since the dog's capa-

Turtles make dull playmates.

Groenendael

bilities were not limited to herding, breeders continued to count this black dog with its medium-long coat as a valuable asset. During World War I these dogs served as messenger, Red Cross, and guard dogs. Agile despite their size (which for males can be as much as 27½ inches tall), they are, like most sheep dogs, adaptable and easy to train (Working: 1–2–3)

BELGIAN MALINOIS: one of three types of Belgian Sheepdogs, the Malinois in its native land had a reputation as a fine herder and a notable guard dog. The Malinois somewhat resembles a German Shepherd but is smaller and, measured at the withers,

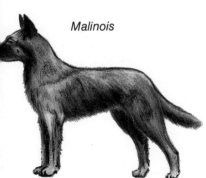
Malinois

should be no less than 22 inches tall and no more than 26. Strong, alert, lively, and easy to train, it is well-proportioned and handsome. Its coat (deep fawn to mahogany with black overlay and black mask and ears) is rather short and straight with a thick undercoat. (Working: 1–3)

BELGIAN TERVUREN: Named after the region in Belgium in which it was bred, this handsome dog is outstanding performer in obedience contests. In body structure it resembles its forefather, the Groenendael, but its coat is fawn-colored with darker patches around the head and chest. Males are about 24 inches in height; bitches a bit less. (Working: 1–2–3)

Tervuren

BELGIUM: The governing canine body is the Union Cynologique Saint-Huber, Avenue de l'Armee, 25, B-1040, Brussels.

BELTON: a coat that is a mixture of white and colored hairs; as, blue belton, liver belton.

BENCHED SHOWS: events at which a dog is assigned a specific bench or cubicle where he remains until his specific breed or event is staged. At Benched Shows dogs and owners are required to remain in attendance until a specified hour, as opposed to Unbenched events where they are excused as soon as a dog has competed in the event in which he was entered. Due to lack of space, Benched Shows are fast going out of fashion.

BERMUDA: Many Americans show their dogs on this lovely island. For information write Bermuda Kennel Club, P.O. 1455, Hamilton, Bermuda.

Bernese Mountain Dog

BERNESE MOUNTAIN DOG: Said to have been brought into Switzerland two thousand years ago by the Roman armies to guard Alpine camps and supply lines, this breed has slowly but steadily increased in popularity with the Swiss, who use it sometimes to pull small carts. Other European countries have recognized its potential, but, surprisingly, it has until recent years been overlooked in Great Britain and the United States. This is even more puzzling because the Bernese has a sunny disposition, closely paralleling that of the Golden Retriever, and its loyalty and devotion to duty make it an ideal pet.

Smallest bitches, if standard, are 21 inches tall; largest dogs, 27½ inches. Weight is about 50 to 70 pounds and the markings are extremely handsome. The dogs are hardy and need little grooming to keep their long coats in good condition. (Working: 1–2–3)

Bichon Frise

BICHON FRISE: Small and white, like the Maltese, this dog is from 8 to 12 inches tall at the shoulder and a lightweight, from 5 to 7 pounds. Despite its pampered beginnings (Henry III of France often carried two or three around in a shallow basket that hung by ribbon straps around his neck), it is a sturdy dog, doesn't mind swimming, and is a particularly good pet for adults. Its coat is double, wavy, silky, and two or more inches long, and requires only daily brushing to keep it in shape. Breed standards allow the dog a dash of apricot, gray, or cream on its ears or body. (Toy: 1–2)

BISCUITS: Puppy biscuits, dog biscuits and a wide variety of related products with other names are composed principally of cereals. All of them provide calories and roughage; they are good for a dog's teeth and gums and keep him occupied and happy. In most cases, the manufacturer adds protiens, carbohydrates, fats and vitamins.

As biscuits, they are intended as dry food for dog to chew on. When ground up and packaged as kibble, water is added. In either case, most owners do not regard biscuits as a complete diet, and supplement them with fish, meat, and additional vitamins.

BITE: the position upper and lower teeth are in when a dog's mouth is closed. The type of bite allowable, level or scissors, undershot or overshot, is determined by each breed's official standard.

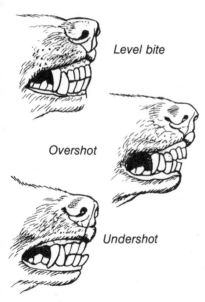

Level bite

Overshot

Undershot

BITING: A dog may bite people for various reasons—pain, fear, panic, aggression, or to protect owners or their property. Dogs bite other dogs for the same reasons and also because of competition in sex or to defend their own property. If bitten by a strange dog, one should contact a physician immediately, for puncture wounds can become infected. Since legal aspects and consequences of dog bites are different in each county, local authorities should be consulted. (See also *rabies*.)

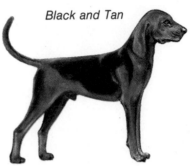

Black and Tan

BLACK AND TAN: One of six Coonhound breeds, the Black and Tan is alone recognized by the AKC, although the *United Kennel Club* does recognize all six. The ancestors of most Coonhounds are Foxhounds, though the Black and Tan has some Bloodhound in his ancestry. Coons (raccoons) are nocturnal animals, and since hunting is generally an autumn and winter sport, these dogs and their owners contend not only with darkness but with icy streams, subfreezing weather, and an adversary strong enough to drown a dog if it is caught in the water.

In a field trial the hunter must be able to follow the voice of his own dog amid a welter of others, following a hot or cold trail. The dog must tree the coon and wait at the base of the tree for its owner and the trial judges to arrive.

The Black and Tan stands from 23 to 27 inches tall at the shoulder, and is strictly a hunter. (Hound: 1–3)

BLANKET: coat color on the back and sides, extending from the neck to, and sometimes including, the tail.

Blaze

BLAZE: a white vertical stripe on the face, generally between the eyes.

BLEU DE GASCOGNE: The *Grand* type (up to 28 inches in height) is rare, one of the few large French hounds still in existence. The *Petit* (up to 22 inches) is seen a bit more often. They resemble Pointers, but have innumerable black spots which give them a blue-mottled appearance. The Bleu de Gascogne Basset is a short-legged version of the same animal.

Bleu de Gascogne

BLINDNESS: Inability to see may involve one eye (monocular blindness) or both eyes (total blindness). Blindness is generally caused by injury or disease of the eye, which interferes with the passage of light impulses to the brain. Common causes are total cataracts, injury to the cornea, or degeneration of the retina or optic nerve. Many of these conditions can be treated if not too advanced. If the furniture is not moved, many blind dogs learn to find their way around the house by their keen senses of smell and hearing, or they may follow another dog—a true Seeing Eye dog.

Prevention: Many apparently minor changes in, or injuries to, the eye can progress rapidly. Check with a veterinarian promptly for diagnosis and treatment.

BLOAT: Seen mostly in large or medium-sized dogs, bloat is a condition in which the stomach rapidly fills with gas and becomes hard and balloonlike. It can prove fatal in two to twelve hours if not treated. Contact a veterinarian immediately, as some cases can be cured by prompt but radical treatment.

BLOCKY: square-headed.

BLOODHOUND: Justly famed for its keen sense of smell, the most acute in the canine world, this big dog with the mournful look is in its element as a tracker. Once it has found the quarry it is trailing, it considers the job finished and (contrary to legend, books, and movies) cannot be persuaded to attack a man or animal. It is also a good-natured and affectionate house dog, but the bigger your

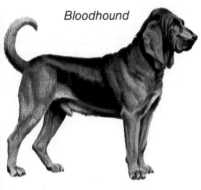

Bloodhound

house, the better. Bloodhounds are from 23 to 27 inches tall, depending on sex, and weigh between 80 to 110 pounds, with show honors largely going to the bigger specimens. Dogs can have a red, black and tan, or liver and tan coat.(Hound: 1–2–3–4)

BLOOD LINE: pedigree showing consecutive generations of breeding with the same ancestry.

BLOOM: coat in perfect condition with proper denseness for the breed.

BLUE MERLE: blue and gray mixed with black so that the coat looks marbled.

BOARDING KENNELS: If you are planning a trip and cannot take your dog with you, a kennel that specializes in boarding (and often grooming) is one answer. If you are unfamiliar with the kennel, you may want to make an appointment to see it and talk with the owner before making a reservation. A well-run establishment should be clean and have runs with access to outdoor areas big enough for medium and large dogs to get some exercise. Boarders should look healthy, and the kennel operator should require evidence that dogs have been immunized within the year against distemper, hepatitis, and leptospirosis. If a dog is on a diet or is a finicky eater, most kennels will be glad to cater to its appetite if the owner provides the diet or pays the added cost of special foods.

A good boarding kennel gives each animal an adequate outdoor area to move about in.

BOBTAIL: a tail docked very short, or a dog without a tail. The name is also applied to the Old English Sheepdog.

BODY TEMPERATURE: best ascertained with a rectal thermometer (stubby). The normal temperature of a dog will range between 101° and 102°, but may go to 102.4° in excitable puppies five to ten weeks old. Puppies under ten days of age are unable to regulate their own body temperature and take on the temperature of their surroundings. They must be kept warm by the dam or by artificial means. The feel of a dog's nose is *not* a reliable guide to its body temperature.

High temperatures (fever) may be due to infections (virus or bacteria), heat stroke, or brain damage. Below normal temperatures may be due to shock, severe infections, or other diseases.

BONE: the circumference of a dog's leg bones. "Good bone" means that the heaviness of a dog's bone is sufficient for it's breed and is in balance with the overall size of the dog.

BONES: see *foods and nutrition*.

BORDER COLLIE: Wherever sheep are raised, this working Collie has been bred for generations for intelligence and trainability, not for its beauty. It is an unexcelled herder, about 18 inches high at the shoulder and weighing up to 45 pounds. It is not recognized in many lands for show purposes, but is nevertheless a distinct type, with a heavy, quite long coat and a bushy tail. (M: 1; Working: 4)

Border Terrier

BORDER TERRIER: The breed originated in the Cheviot Hills forming the border between England and Scotland, where it was used to hunt native foxes that harried and killed lambs. The dog is wiry and strong, a tireless worker, and adaptable. Since there are few foxes around these days, this courageous little fellow (weight 11½ to 15½ pounds) has taken happily to family life instead. It is loyal, good with children, and is easy to take care of because its coat (red, grizzle and tan, blue and tan, or wheaten) does not have to be stripped. (Terrier: 1–2–3–4)

BORZOI: This magnificent animal, for centuries a court favorite in Russia, evolved when Arabian Greyhounds were crossed with long-legged steppe Collies with thick, wavy coats. The result was a dog that had great speed for

Border Collie

Borzoi

hunting and could also withstand severe winter weather. In pairs, matched for size and speed, they were used to run down wolves during hunts that were displays of style and elegance. During Queen Victoria's reign the Czar presented her with several of these strong, speedy hounds. English aristocrats proved as devoted to the breed as their Russian cousins were, but it was not until about the turn of the century that the dogs arrived in the United States. They remain special animals for rather special owners, since they are as much as 31 inches tall, weigh up to 105 pounds, have large appetites, and require a great deal of exercise. (Hound: 1–2–3–4)

BOSSY: a term referring not to personality traits but to over-development of shoulder muscles.

BOSTON TERRIER: A true American dog, this breed apparently resulted from crosses between Bulldogs and Bull Terriers and was developed for pit fighting in and around Boston. Having long ago forgotten the purposes for which it was bred, it has become a gentle house pet and a good companion.

Dogs are judged in three weight classes: lightweight, middle-weight, and heavyweight, and range from under 15 pounds for the lightest to 25 pounds for the heaviest. Brindle with white markings is the preferred coat color, though black with white is permitted.

Owners who buy a female puppy with an eye to breeding her should be aware that almost all litters have to be delivered by Caesarean section, since the head size of the puppies makes normal delivery virtually impossible. (Nonsporting: 1–3–4; Utility: 2)

Boston Terrier

BORDER TERRIER: The breed originated in the Cheviot Hills forming the border between England and Scotland, where it was used to hunt native foxes that harried and killed lambs. The dog is wiry and strong, a tireless worker, and adaptable. Since there are few foxes around these days, this courageous little fellow (weight 11½ to 15½ pounds) has taken happily to family life instead. It is loyal, good with children, and is easy to take care of because its coat (red, grizzle and tan, blue and tan, or wheaten) does not have to be stripped. (Terrier: 1–2–3–4) inches tall, have rough, wiry, thick coats, which can range from fawn

Bouvier des Flandres

to black in color, or pepper and salt, or gray and brindle. Weight averages from 60 to 70 pounds. (Working: 1–2–3)

BOXER: The Boxer was methodically bred for security purposes along German borders during the last century, resulting in an animal that could scent smuggled contraband, guard land areas, attack interlopers, and generally make itself useful for police work. Before that, its ancestors were doubtless used for pit fighting and bull baiting. Despite their guard-dog abilities, they are splendid family pets and good playmates for children. The Boxer is a medium-sized dog (21 to 25 inches at the shoulder, 60 to 70 pounds) with a medium-sized appetite. Fawn and brindle are acceptable colors.

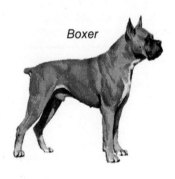

Boxer

For etymology students, the dog's name was bestowed on it because it begins to play or fight with its front paws, using motions much like those of a boxer. (Working: 1–2–3: Nonsporting: 4)

BRACE: a pair of dogs of the same breed.

BRACHYCEPHALIC: designating the shape of the head of such breeds as bulldogs, who have round heads and pushed-in faces.

BRAZIL: The Brazil Kennel Club, Caixa Postal 1468, Rio de Janeiro, is the national authority.

BREECH BIRTH: see *whelping*.

BREED: Of upward of 800 separate species of dogs, only a relatively small percentage are recognized by kennel clubs throughout the world for registration and show purposes, and these vary considerably from country to country. In Great Britain, for example, approximately 160 breeds are recognized, including all variations within a specific breed. In the United States, Australia, and Canada, fewer breeds and variations are recognized.

Great Britain classifies recognized breeds as Sporting (Hounds, Gundogs, and Terriers) and Nonsporting (Utility, Working, and Toys). In the United States breeds are divided into Sporting, Hound, Working, Terrier, Toy, and Nonsporting classes. Certain other dogs are classified as "miscellaneous," but may eventually be admitted into a specific class, if certain registration requirements are met.

Over any two or three year period the kennel clubs of various countries admit a few new breeds for registration and eliminate those breeds for which no registrations have been made within a given period of time.

BREEDER: a person who has on his premises one or more bitches which are mated for commercial purposes—for sale as pets, as guide dogs, or to produce potential show, field, or obedience dogs. Most serious breeders are also interested in the genetics aspect of breed improvements.

BREEDING: Except for Toy breeds, in which the pelvis, once set, may be too narrow to allow whelping without difficulty, most bitches should not be bred until they are fully mature—up to two years for big breeds. Bitches should be in top condition, wormed before mating, x-rayed for hip dysplasia if they are of a susceptible breed, and checked to make certain there are no abnormalities that would make whelping undesirable. A suitable stud should be selected in advance and arrangements as to fee and site of breeding made well ahead of the bitch's expected heat. Bitches are generally most receptive to mating from ten to thirteen days after the first signs of vaginal bleeding, indicating heat, are noted.

Linebreeding—mating of animals which have at least one common ancestor within the first three generations—is acceptable. Inbreeding—mating of brother to sister or mother to son—is for experts only, since the parents' worst as well as best qualities will be prominent in the offspring.

Bred to fight wolves in their native Anatolia, these Karabash dogs make endlessly patient home companions.

BREED STANDARD: a "profile" of an ideal specimen of each breed by which dogs are measured against others of their breed in the show ring. Faults that disqualify a dog in the ring do not disqualify it for field or obedience work, and certainly do not bar it as a pet. For the protection of the breed, dogs with serious faults, as designated by the breed standard, should never be bred.

BRINDLE: an even mixture of black hairs with those of a lighter color, generally brown, gray, or tan.

BRISKET: the front of the body below the chest, between the forelegs and nearest to the ribs.

Briard

Brittany Spaniel

BRIARD: Workers whose lineage goes back to a very old race of French dogs pictured on tapestries dating from the fourteenth century, Briards have been cattle and sheep herders, guardians of property, and pack animals for carrying ammunition and first-aid supplies in wartime. Representatives of the breed have an extraordinarily keen sense of hearing and, while not quick learners, remember well once the message gets through.

A big dog (22 to 27 inches tall at the shoulder and from 70 to 80 pounds in weight), the Briard stays close to home, rarely barks, and has a hard, slightly wavy, stiff coat which is both water- and mud-proof. It can be any solid color except white, but the darker it is,

the better for show purposes. (Working: 1–2–3)

BRITTANY SPANIEL: Alone among Spaniels, this dog is, when hunting, a Pointer who is often out of sight of the hunter. It points on a hidden bird and keeps the bird from escaping until the hunter comes up within gun range. Originally used to hunt woodcock in Brittany, it is equally adept at pheasant hunting in the United States and is an excellent retriever.

The Brittany is leggier and has a shorter coat than most Spaniels. For showing, it must be from 17½ to 20½ inches tall at the shoulder, weigh from 30 to 40 pounds, and have a dark-orange and white or liver and white coat. It is often born tailless, and if it isn't, must have the tail docked to a maximum length of four inches. (Sporting: 1–3)

BROOD BITCH: a female dog kept for breeding purposes. She should be a good specimen of her breed in type and temperament, but not necessarily a show dog. She must be kept in hard condition and not be overweight. She needs a liberal, well-balanced diet and plenty of exercise, and must be free of parasites (internal and external). She should be at least one year of age (small breeds) and two years if a large breed. To maintain top condition, she should not be bred more than once a year.

BRUSH: a bushy tail.

BRUSSELS GRIFFON: A true rags-to-riches dog, the Brussels Griffon worked its way up in its native Belgium from rat-catching in stables to riding the front seat of hansom cabs with a distinguished owner. These days, the Brussels Griffon comes in two coat varieties: rough (the result of crosses with Affenpinschers and so-called Belgian street dogs) and smooth (Pug and Griffon crosses).

As a puppy, the Brussels Griffon is awkward and self-conscious with strangers; at all ages it is somewhat stubborn, particularly about leash training, which must

Brussels Griffon

be begun very early if it is to be effective. Bitches are difficult to breed, and litters are likely to be small in number as well as in size. A variety of coat colors are acceptable for the Brussels, who weighs a maximum of 12 pounds and is often much lighter. (Toy: 1–2–3–4)

Bulldog

BULLDOG: In the days when it was used to fight against bulls, the Bulldog's job was to bury its tremendously strong jaws in the bull's hide and hang on. The British outlawed these contests early in the nineteenth century, and one of the great turnabouts in dog history resulted. Breeders who valued the dog's courage, strength, and essential dignity managed in a few generations to breed out its ferocity. Today, the Bulldog is a fine pet—fun-loving, devoted, friendly, and easygoing.

A medium-sized dog (males weigh 50 pounds, females 40), the Bulldog has an odd, rolling gait and is not noted for its beauty-pageant potential, but it does have a superb character. It comes in a wide range of colors—brindles of all sorts, solid white, red, or fawn, piebald —indeed, anything but black. Its fine, smooth, short coat calls for a minimum of grooming. (Non-sporting: 1–3–4: Utility:2)

Bullmastiff

BULLMASTIFF: Members of the British nobility in the nineteenth century customarily lived on large estates where they kept herds of deer and other game for pleasure and sport. To guard their animals, they hired gamekeepers who needed a dog that was fast, big, silent when poachers were about, and that would attack and hold on command without mortally wounding the victim. By crossing the Mastiff and the Bulldog, landowners got exactly what they sought.

Since such estates have given way to smaller, unfenced holdings, the Bullmastiff, who can be any color of brindle, red, or fawn, has changed its field of operation to guard and watchdog activities. Because of its size (from 24 to 27 inches tall and from 90 to 130 pounds), it is perhaps not an ideal house pet. (Working: 1–2–3; Non-sporting: 4)

BULL TERRIER: a cross between a Bulldog and a Terrier, this dog was bred originally to fight other dogs, with bets laid on the outcome. Sports became more civilized, and the Bull Terrier along with them. Today, this unusual dog with its football-shaped head is affectionate and lively, likes to play with children, and is a fine companion.. Somewhere along the line it lost its antipathy for other dogs as well. At dog shows it gets along with its competitors just as well as other breeds do.

Bull Terriers are predominantly white or colored. Color can be any shade and can be mixed with white as long as the basic color predominates. Weight ranges from 25 to 60 pounds. (Terrier: 1–2–3–4)

Bull Terrier

BULL TERRIER, MINIATURE: Identical in history, heritage, and temperament to the Bull Terrier, this is simply a dog that weighs 20 pounds or less and must not be more than 14 inches tall. (M: 1; Terrier: 2)

BURN: injury to the skin caused by dry heat, such as a radiator or hot cinders; wet heat, as boiling fluids or steam; or chemicals, such as acids or alkalies. Burns are catagorized as first, second, or third degree.

First-degree or superficial burns: Only the external layers of the skin are damaged. The area appears red and sensitive, but heals rapidly without scar formation. Cold tea is a useful home treatment.

Second-degree burns: The superficial and middle layers of the skin are killed, including the hair follicles and blood vessels. If a large area of the body is involved, the dog may go into shock, followed by infection. Healing leaves a permanent scar on which hair never regrows. Prompt veterinary treatment is essential.

Third-degree burns: The entire thickness of the skin is involved. The area dies, shrinks, and exposes the underlying tissues. Shock and infection are usual. As a first-aid measure it is essential to keep the animal warm, cover the burned area with a clean towel, and seek veterinary help at once.

BURR: an irregular formation of the inside of the ear.

BUTTERFLY DOG: see *Papillon*.

BUTTERFLY NOSE: a nose of more than one color, generally black with pink spots.

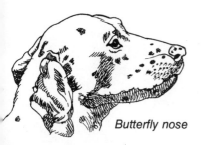

Butterfly nose

BUTTON EAR: an ear with a folded-forward flap. The tip lies close to the head and covers the opening. The tip of the ear points toward the eye.

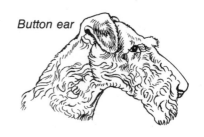

Button ear

BUYING A DOG: There are almost as many ways of acquiring a dog as there are breeds, and generalities in this area are dangerous. Here are the most common methods:

1. From a kennel. Most kennels specialize in a single breed and have bitches of proven quality on the premises.

2. From a private family. Puppies raised in a good home and whelped by the family pet will have many qualities you want.

3. From a pet shop in one's neighborhood. Make certain, however, that the shop has been in business for some time and enjoys a good reputation.

4. From a humane society shelter. This is the least expensive method, costing little or nothing, and is acceptable if you are not interested in owning a thoroughbred animal and willing to run the risk that the animal has neuroses or undesirable characteristics which perhaps stem from an unhappy puppyhood. To this note of caution, it should be added that thousands upon thousands of owners have acquired delightful animals from shelters.

Whatever method is chosen in purchasing a dog here are several points to bear in mind:

1. Don't buy a puppy that has diarrhea, a runny nose, watering eyes, ears that are sore or smell, or whose litter mates show any of these symptoms.
2. Don't buy a puppy that snaps at your hand when you try to pick it up or pet it, or that shrinks away from you or hides under something when you approach it. Puppies in sound health are friendly and curious.
3. "AKC or KC Registered" means that the litter is registered and that the puppy is eligible for individual registration. Any seller of dogs who claims his puppies are AKC registerable must give the buyers an AKC application form filled out and signed by the seller, or a signed bill of sale or written

Bought in Britain by members of the Dog Franciers Club of U.S.A., these pups are enroute to America. Exportation of pure-bred dogs has long been a thriving English industry.

statement giving the dog's full breeding information at the time of sale. As the AKC warns, "Do not accept a promise of later identification." It is up to you to complete and send to the AKC the application form and the required fee in order to register the dog you have bought.

4. Don't forget to find out whether the puppy has been wormed and had the necessary inoculations before you take it home.
5. Don't buy any puppy less than six weeks old. Seven weeks old is better; eight is best.

As to the breed of dog you select, clichés are suspect. For example, "all dogs need exercise." Setters and other hunting dogs do, but in tens of thousands of homes throughout the world there are small dogs (and large ones) who don't go out in the "fresh air" twice a year—and who are living blissfully happy lives.

In choosing a dog, therefore, the factors to be considered are (a) your individual preference; (b) where you live; (c) how you live; (d) the activities the dog will pursue.

Show Dogs and Field Trial Dogs: If you want a dog that may, when mature, qualify for these specialized activities, and if you have time, patience, and money, consult a breeder who has had significant success in one of these areas. Be prepared to pay a premium price for the puppy.

A breeder who tells you that the puppy he wants to sell you is a born champion is not telling the truth. It is impossible to tell whether a seven-week-old pup will grow up to have the characteristics necessary to make it top dog in the show or field world.

C

CAESAREAN SECTION: a surgical operation in which live puppies are removed from the dam through an incision in the abdomen. Caesareans are performed for any condition in which the puppies cannot be delivered through the birth canal, e.g., large-headed pups, uncorrectable presentations in which the canal is blocked, uterine inertia (inability of the womb to contract and expel the puppy), or deformed pelvis.

Modern techniques have made this a relatively safe operation if not delayed too long. The dam can usually nurse her own puppies after she has recovered from the anesthesia.

CAIRN TERRIER: This breed was so named because it worked at finding and killing foxes and otters in the cairns, or piles of rocks and stones, of the Scottish Western Highlands and the Isle of Skye off

Scotland's west coast. If there is no such work for it to do, you may still consider him an ideal pet. The Cairn weighs a maximum of 14 pounds, is not more than 10 inches tall at the withers, has a hard, short coat that needs virtually no grooming, is active and sturdy but not a fighter, and learns quickly. Any color but white is approved at dog shows. Dark ears, muzzle, and tail tip are plusses. (Terrier: 1–2–3–4)

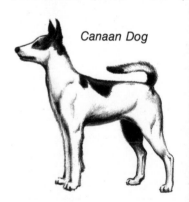

Canaan Dog

Cairn Terrier

CANAAN DOG: Dating back to pre-biblical times, legend has it that Queen Jezebel had a Canaan dog tied to her throne with a golden chain. During recent decades Israeli breeders domesticated the wild and semi-wild animals who for

centuries had made their home in the Negev desert. During the past thirty years Canaans have served in increasing numbers in mine-detection work, and as guardians of Israeli borders, factories, homes and children. Above all, they are used as seeing-eye dogs. A medium sized animal, the Canaan is hardy and amiable. Weight ranges widely, from 35 to 55 pounds, and height at the shoulder is between 18½ and 22½ inches. Almost any color but grey or brindle is acceptable. (Working: 2)

CANADIAN KENNEL CLUB: Founded in 1888, it is the national authority and, as such, registers dogs and supervises shows as well as field and obedience trials. Unlike the United States, member clubs are not admitted to membership, only individuals who have shown and proved their lasting interest in the welfare of dogs.

Breed standards in Canada parallel those below the border, but several breeds recognized in the United States are not on the Canadian roster, while others, like the Eskimo Dog and Nova Scotia Duck Tolling Dog, are recognized exclusively in the Dominion.

Both judges and dog owners from both countries participate with increasing frequency in one another's shows and trials since the procedures followed are almost identical. Address: 111 Eglinton Avenue, Toronto 12, Ontario, Canada.

CANCER: see *tumors*.

CANINES: the two fanglike upper and two lower long teeth.

CANKER: an inflammation of the ear due to infection. External can-

kers may be treated at home if one follows the instructions of a veterinarian, while internal infections most probably call for expert treatment. Symptom of internal infection: a thick yellow or brownish discharge with an offensive odor.

CARDIGAN WELSH CORGI: The word *Corgi* means dog in Celtic and the two popular breeds, Cardigan and Pembroke, bear a superficial resemblance to one another but quite possibly stemmed from different ancestors. Both breeds were adept at cattle driving and today both make lively and intelligent guardians and pets.

The Cardigan's head is foxy in appearance; he is long-tailed with ears rounded at the top, and his front is slightly bowed. Body length, from nose to tail-tip, varies from 36 to 44 inches. Height is around 12 inches and almost any color but pure white or predominantly white is acceptable. Over the years the Cardigan has been somewhat less popular than the Pembroke. (Working: 1–2–3–4)

Cardigan Welsh Corgi

CAREERS FOR DOGS: There are a variety of commercial possibilities for trained, photogenic dogs. The stage and motion pictures are perhaps the oldest of these.

Rin Tin Tin was to motion pictures what Lassie was to TV. This twenty-year-old photograph of the great Rin Tin Tin shows him on the Hollywood set with a chimpanzee friend

If interested in these possibilities, you must be willing to travel with your dog to the studio or location where the filming is to be done. Your dog must be well disciplined and capable of learning a new routine quickly; amenable to loud noises, bright lights, endlessly patient and, above all, a complete extrovert that likes everybody it meets. Since the dog is almost always a bit player and not a star, it cannot be temperamental if it hopes to be regularly employed.

Champion dogs and top brood bitches can create considerable income for owners, of course, by producing puppies for sale to the general public.

Television uses dogs not only for one-shot or continuing programs but for commercials advertising all sorts of products and services. Magazine and newspaper ads and advertising posters are other possibilities. Many successful canine models have agents. In major cities, they are listed in the telephone directory. Fees vary, depending on the nature of the job. The dog's agent collects the fee, keeps an agreed-upon percentage, and delivers the balance to the owner.

Dog models play an increasingly important role in magazine and newspaper advertisements.

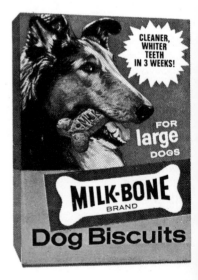

CARE OF A SICK DOG: depends on the nature of the sickness. Follow your veterinarian's instructions carefully. Write down the most important points. Handle the dog gently and keep it clean and comfortable. In many diseases T.L.C. (tender loving care) is a most important factor in medical treatment for successful recovery.

CARIBBEAN KENNEL CLUB: The address is P.O. 737, Port of Spain, Trinidad, W.I.

CAR SICKNESS: Vomiting caused by motion may be due to vibrations on the ears or brain or to nervousness. The simple remedies used for children may be given to dogs.

Prevention: Do not feed the dog before a long journey. Take young puppies for a short ride as often as possible and make the trip fun. Many dogs become car sick because they associate the ride with a trip to the veterinarian or kennel.

CASTRATION: surgical removal of both testicles in the male dog. Such an operation is necessary in some medical conditions and may sometimes calm an overaggressive dog.

CATARACT: see *eye disease*.

CAT FOOT: a compact rounded foot.

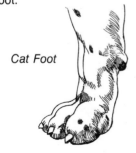

Cat Foot

*Cavalier
King Charles Spaniel*

CAVALIER KING CHARLES SPANIEL: A rollicking dog who makes a sturdy playmate, the King Charles is directly descended from the little Spaniels seen in art masterpieces dating back four centuries. Named after Charles II, who gave his beribboned beauties the run of the palace, the breed almost died out at one time, but of recent years has come back into great popularity in England and is beginning to be known in America. They are active and graceful dogs, weighing from 10 to 18 pounds, and are divided into four color categories: Black and Tan, Ruby, Blenheim, and Tri-Color. (M: 1; Toy: 2–3–4)

Cesky Terrier

CESKY TERRIER: This short-legged and long-tailed (up to 8 inches) little fellow originated in Bohemia and may some day be numbered among Czechoslo-

Ramacon Swashbuckler, a German Shepherd (Alsatian in Great Britain) beside a cup representing the Supreme Championship of Cruft's Show.

vakian exports. It somewhat resembles a cut-down Kerry Blue although its gray-blue or brownish coat is wavy. The Cesky is amiable and a good companion.

CHAINING, CHAINS: see *confinement*.

CHALLENGE CERTIFICATE: In most countries in the British Commonwealth three C.C.'s make a Champion, and the Challenge Certificates must be awarded by three different judges at championship shows. C.C.'s in Great Britian are rigidly limited by the number of dogs shown in a specific breed; thus, there are fewer than forty sets of Certificates for the most popular breeds each year, and no Certificates at all for breeds that are sparsely represented. As a result, a British owner of an *Affenpinscher* or a *Glen of Imaal Terrier* has no way to make his dog a Champion unless there is enough competition to induce the Kennel Club to issue at least one set of C.C.'s. In Great Britian as well, there is no special class for existing Champions and to win a C.C. a contender must defeat all contenders of his or her sex *and* competing Champions as well.

CHAMPIONSHIPS, U.S. and CANADA: These are awarded on a point system, and it takes 10 points to make a Canadian Champion and 15 to gain the title in the United States. Points in the United States are based upon a geographical zoning system:

1. The number of dogs in a given breed registered annually in the zone.

2. The number of dogs of the same breed who compete in the zone.

3. The number of shows given each year in the zone.

Points range from 5 down to 1 and depend on the three factors cited above. Thus, in Zone 1, the Northern and Eastern United States, a German Shepherd must defeat seventy-three other dogs and a Saint Bernard bitch must defeat fifty-six others of her sex to win 5 points; at the same show, a Belgian Terverun dog or a Skye Terrier bitch can gain 5 points by defeating only five others of the same breed and sex.

Only the winning dog and the winning bitch can gain points, but, as opposed to regulations in Great Britain, established Champions are a separate category and compete only to determine Best of Breed.

Canadian shows differ from those held below the border in several respects: to win a Champion's title, points must be awarded by at least three different judges; even if a dog is awarded Best of Breed, it must participate in group judging against other winners in its classification—Sporting

Having won upwards of twenty-five best-in-show awards with Great Danes and Boxers, Mrs. Joe Longo of Harrison, New York, has been winning championship awards in the obedience ring. She is shown above with some of her trophies and with her obedient poodles.

or Toy or Hounds, etc.; finally, to gain points, it must either defeat at least one dog of its own breed or place in a group where five different breeds are competing.

CHEEKY: cheeks that are rounded and full.

Cherry nose

CHERRY NOSE: a pink nose that is considered a fault (often disqualifying) for a breed, e.g., the Fox Terrier.

CHESAPEAKE BAY RETRIEVER: No match for his relative the Labrador when it comes to speed and style in field trials, this dog is nonetheless a rugged and dependable performer for duck hunting, particularly in subzero weather and in rough water. Its ancestors arrived in an English ship that was wrecked off the Maryland coast more than 160 years ago. Two puppies aboard (probably Newfoundlands) were

Chesapeake Bay Retriever

rescued, and then bred to local gun dogs to produce the Chesapeake.

The Chesapeake is a big dog weighing from 55 to 75 pounds and from 21 to 26 inches tall. Its short, thick outer coat is oily and sheds water easily, while its undercoat is dense to keep it warm when weather and water are cold. The coat can be wavy but not curly. It is most successful as a duck hunter if its coat is the color of dead grass, though it can be darker, including chocolate but not black. (Sporting: 1–2–3)

Smooth Chihuahua

Long-coated Chihuahua

CHIHUAHUA: The world's tiniest dog, this breed's history probably goes back to the Toltecs and Aztecs, but the first examples of the modern breed hailed from the Mexican state of Chihuahua in the mid-nineteenth century. It is more popular in the smooth-coated variety than in the long-coated one, but both have a growing army of boosters. It is unusual not alone for its size but also for its "mol-

56

lers"—an area where the skull bones are not joined, as in newborn human babies—and for the fact that when it comes to canine company, it is very choosy, preferring other Chihuahuas. It is a digger and hunter and fancies itself as a fierce and protective watchdog. Whether smooth or long-haired, its preferred weight is 2 to 4 pounds, and its coat can be solid, splashed, or marked any color. (Toy 1–2–3–4.)

CHILE: The address of the offices of the Kennel Club de Chile is Casilla 1704, Valparaiso.

CHINA EYE: an eye that is clear blue.

CHINESE CRESTED DOG: see *hairless dogs*.

CHINESE FIGHTING DOG: What looks like a baby hippopotamus, has canine teeth shaped like a scythe, stiff bristles like a pig, attacks other dogs with the ferocity of a wild boar, but loves people like any other dog? Answer: a Chinese Fighting Dog. In China it has been battling other dogs for centuries, and since that's what it enjoys best, it is listed here only as an example of one dog that is not an ideal pet.

CHOKE CHAINS: see *collars*.

CHOKING: often caused by a foreign object lodged in a dog's throat or esophagus (gullet) or trachea (windpipe), and which interferes with normal breathing. Bones, marbles, and stones are common obstructions. As a first-aid measure the owner may attempt to remove the object by holding the dog up by its hind legs. Many owners confuse choking

with coughing and other diseases of the throat and trachea—for example, kennel cough or tracheitis or bronchitis.

CHOPS: pendulous flesh of lips and jaws, like the bulldog's.

CHOREA: an involuntary twitch of one or more groups of muscles. Chorea is not painful and in mild cases not disabling. It is a frequent complication of canine distemper.

Chow Chow

CHOW CHOW: This breed apparently traces its ancestry back more than two thousand years in China, and may well be the ancestor of the Samoyed and the Pomeranian. The Chow Chow came to England in the late nineteenth century and has flourished to a degree in the Western world ever since. It is the only known canine with a blue-black tongue. Its name is probably derived from early sea captains who described their ships' mixed cargoes from the Orient in pidgin English as "chow-chose."

Breed standards call for a "massive" dog without specifying height or weight, though typical specimens range from 18 to 20 inches in height and from 50 to 60 pounds in weight. The Chow Chow can be any clear, solid color with

Two Chow Chow pups line up at the milk bar.

lighter shadings, but without patches. It is generally a devoted "one-family dog." If a member of the family is with the dog, it will be polite to visitors but away from a watchful human eye it may prove distinctly unfriendly to strangers. (Nonsporting: 1–3–4; Utility: 2)

CLASSES AT DOG SHOWS: Throughout the world, dogs are generally divided by sex for breed judging. In the United States, breeds are divided into Puppy Classes, Novice, Bred-by-Exhibitor, American-bred Dogs, and Open Classes. Winners in each Class compete with other Class Winners of the same sex for the title of Winners Dog or Winners Bitch. The two finalists compete against Champions of record for the Best of Breed Award.

In Great Britain, there are up to twenty separate Classes, ranging from Puppy, Junior, Maiden and Novice to Veterans. Included are such intriguing Class names as Tyro, Debutante and Graduate.

Dog shows in Great Britain are divided into Members Shows and Open Shows, and a Championship can only be gained at an Open Show.

Classes in Canada are as follows: Junior and Senior Puppy, Novice, Canadian-bred, Bred by Exhibitor and Open.

Rules are similar to those in the United States, although there are some breed technicalities that are different and special awards for Canadian-bred dogs in various classes.

In most dog shows throughout the English speaking world, prize money is also given to the winners.

Since the rules and regulations governing dog shows are somewhat complicated and since qualifications vary widely from country to country, it is best to consult a local kennel club if one decides to show a dog in competition.

CLEFT PALATE: The hard palate, or roof of the mouth, is a thick sheet of bone that separates the mouth from the nasal passages and sinuses. When "cleft," it is incomplete and leaves a hole between the mouth and the nose. This condition is often congenital (present at birth). The newborn puppy is unable to suck because the milk gets into its nose and lungs.

If the puppy can be kept alive (with tube feeding) for several weeks, corrective surgery may be considered in a few cases.

The condition is not uncommon in short-nosed dogs (Pugs, Bos-

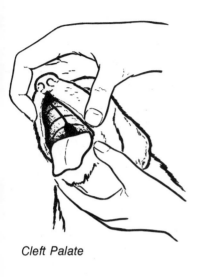

Cleft Palate

tons, etc.) and may be complicated by hairlip.

CLIPPING: Some dogs are clipped for a number of reasons: so as to be neat and clean; when they are suffering from skin ailments so that medication can be easily applied; and for show purposes as in the case of Poodles, who are trimmed *and* shaved. Many breeds, particularly those who shed their undercoat in warm weather, should *not* be clipped; Terriers, for example, are plucked or stripped in most cases.

CLODDY: low, rather heavy, thickset.

A Standard Poodle, stylishly clipped for showing.

CLOSE-COUPLED: comparatively short from withers to hipbones.

Clumber Spaniel

CLUMBER SPANIEL: Sedate is the word for this long, low, powerful-looking dog, which has a surprising weight range from 35 pounds for bitches to 65 pounds for dogs. British standards call for heavier animals in both sexes. In England, where Clumbers originated, there was plenty of the kind of game they were required to hunt, so neither they nor their leisurely paced owners had to hurry. Probably crossed over the years with Basset Hounds, they are slow but sure and make excellent retrievers. They are white dogs with lemon or orange markings, the fewer the better. (Sporting: 1–2–3)

COAT: hair covering animal's body.

COBBY: compact, short-bodied.

COLD NOSE: Despite many often repeated claims, a cold nose is no indication of whether or not a dog is in good health.

COLLAR: marking around the neck, most often white.

COLLARS: As soon as you bring a new puppy home (ideally when it is eight weeks old), it is time to teach it to live with a collar for short periods of time every day. The collar should be loose enough to be comfortable, but not so loose it can slip over the puppy's head. Buy a larger size as often as the dog out-

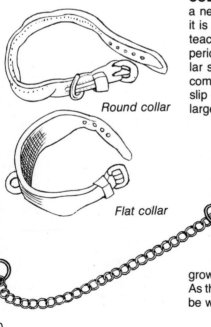

Round collar

Flat collar

Choke chain collar

grows the one it has been wearing. As the dog matures, collars should be worn at all times when outside the house, on leash or off. Most owners choose to attach to the collar identification tags in case the dog strays from home, its license, and a tag indicating that it has received rabies vaccine. A proper fitting collar will not irritate a dog's neck unless he is allergic to some substance in the collar, in which case another should be substituted. Round collars are best for long-haired dogs, flat ones for short-haired animals.

Many owners prefer a choke chain collar to a leather one. This is nothing more than a length of chain with a loop on each end. If you hold the chain by one loop, pick up the other loop, and drop a length of chain through the loop in your right hand, you will wind up with a circle of chain you can slip over your dog's head. If you attach a leash to the free loop or slip your finger through it, you have an ideal training collar. If you are giving the dog a command and it fails to obey, a tug tightens the collar. If you release the pull on the ring, the collar immediately falls loose around the neck. Make sure the circle of chain is long enough to fit easily over the dog's head. Today, nylon collars are also becoming popular.

COLLIE: *ROUGH:* A working sheep dog from northern Scotland, this breed was little known in studbooks or dog shows until just over a hundred years ago. Queen Victoria saw some of these big dogs with their elegant coats, frills, and manes at Balmoral Castle and took an immediate fancy to them. What the Queen did was likely to be imitated, and the dog soon

Rough Collie

became popular as a pet not only in Great Britian but in the United States. A truly beautiful animal, fastidious, reliable, and a born protector, it can be sable and white, tricolor, blue merle, or white for show purposes in the United States. In England there are no color standards for the breed. At the shoulder dogs range from 22 to 26 inches tall and weigh from 50 to 75 pounds; bitches are somewhat less. (Working: 1–2–3–4)

Smooth Collie

COLLIE, *SMOOTH:* This breed probably originated in northern England, though it was equally well known in Scotland. It differs only from its long-haired cousin in that

61

The coat color of this litter of Collie pups will gradually lighten.

its coat is short, dense, and smooth. As a worker, however, it was used to drive livestock to market rather than as a sheepherder. It has always been less popular as a pet than the rough Collie, but since it has great aptitude for obedience training, it is gaining in favor. (Working: 1–2–3–4)

CONCUSSION: an injury to the brain due to trauma (a blow or fall on the head). Concussion causes an accumulation of fluid (blood or serum) to form under the bony scalp and put pressure on the underlying soft brain tissue. It may or may not cause unconsciousness, and generally clears up by itself with rest and conservative treatment.

CONDITION: the state of a dog's health. An active dog in proper weight for his build, in good muscle tone, and with a clean, healthy coat is considered in good condition.

CONFINEMENT: Since companionship is essential to the well-being of most dogs, they should be kept in confinement for as short periods as possible. An animal who is chained or locked-up for many hours becomes bored and frustrated, and may well turn into a biter, compulsive barker or a destructive animal. If you must leave your dog indoors for considerable periods of time and he cannot be trusted alone in the home, it may be best to keep him in a wire crate of appropriate size. A possible alternative is to confine the dog in a suitable area, such as a kitchen or bathroom, by putting a portable gate across the entrance.

Outdoors, to protect the dog from roaming and from street hazards, it is recommended that a fenced-in area be provided where the dog can enjoy a fair amount of unrestricted activity.

Any outdoor area of confinement should be in a location where some shade is always available. A container of fresh water should be readily accessible to the dog at all times.

Wire cage for travel or home use.

CONFORMATION: the manner in which a dog is structured and the relationship of one part of the body to another.

CONJUNCTIVITIS: see *eye diseases and injuries.*

CONSTIPATION: a condition in which the dog is unable to move its bowels, leading to an accumulation of fecal material in the rectum and colon. Constipation may be caused by incorrect diet, from swallowing bones, or by diseases of the rectum or prostate. Laxatives *can be dangerous.* Simple cases can be treated by insertion of a glycerine suppository or a low-grade enema. If this causes pain or does not relieve the condition, see a veterinarian promptly.

COPROPHAGY: the eating of excrement. It is a symptom and not a disease. It may be caused by indigestion, inadequate diet, parasites (especially hookworms), boredom, or other conditions. Coprophagy is sometimes due to faulty housebreaking. A puppy who associates the sight of a bowel movement with severe punishment may eat the movement to remove the evidence. Thus, the owner's approach is of key importance.

CORGI: see *Cardigan Welsh Corgi* and *Pembroke Welsh Corgi.*

COUGH: A sign of irritation or pressure in the trachea, bronchi, or lungs, coughing may result from:

(1) Accumulation of mucus in bronchial passages or lungs (colds, bronchitis).

(2) Pressure in the chest from tumors or parasites.

(3) Some forms of heart disease.

An exact diagnosis is essential for effective treatment.

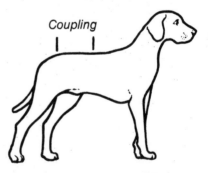

Coupling

COUPLING: the part of the body between the last rib and hip joint. Depending on the length, an animal is considered short- or long-coupled.

COURSING: the sport, dating back many centuries, of chasing and running down animals with sight hounds—Afghans, Greyhounds, and the like. Coursing trials are still held in a number of countries.

Cow-hock

COW-HOCKED: when hocks are not parallel and hock joints turn in towards each other, with feet turning out.

CRABBING: when a dog moves forward and at a sideway angle he is said to be *crabbing*. Crabbing results when the reach of the hindquarters exceeds the length of stride of the forequarters.

CRANK TAIL: a short tail carried down and at an angle, and resembling a crank handle.

CROPPING: see *ear cropping*.

CROSSBREED: any dog whose parents were of different breeds, either deliberately, as in the cockapoo (a cross between a Cocker Spaniel and a Poodle), or accidentally.

CROSSING OVER: putting one front foot down ahead of, and to the right or left of, the other foot.

CROUP: the section above the hind legs from the hipbone to the tail.

CROWN: the topmost part of the skull.

CRUELTY: see *humane societies*.

CRY: the voice of a hound.

CRYPTORCHIDISM: technically, a condition in which neither testicle is present in the scrotum of the male dog. The term is often used loosely to describe the condition of having one testicle in the scrotum and the other in the abdomen or inguinal passage—actually called monorchidism. In young excitable dogs the testicles may become spastic and be withdrawn into the abdomen under stress.

Cryptorchidism is often, but not always, congenital (passed from one generation to the next). Therefore, monorchids should not be used in a breeding program, although they are often fertile. True cryptorchids are always sterile.

Most kennel clubs regard monorchidism and cryptorchidism as causes for disqualification in show dogs.

CRUFT'S DOG SHOW: This most important event of the year in the British dog world attracts fifty thousand visitors each February. Charles Cruft, a traveler (or salesman) for Spratt's dog biscuits, launched the show in 1891 and annually delighted Londoners with it thereafter. After his death in 1938, the Kennel Club acquired the rights to the show from his widow, and now conducts it in keeping with KC regulations that bar dog shows for private gain. The number of entries and lack of space have combined to restrict entries to former champions and to dogs who have won first- or second-place awards at championship shows during the preceding year. To be named supreme champion at Cruft's, therefore, is the dream of breeders everywhere.

Tolly, a British-bred Basset Hound, proudly displays his awards and ribbons.

CURLY-COATED RETRIEVER: A dog who can't bark up its family tree with authority, the Curly-Coat's ancestry is a mystery. It is perhaps descended from English or Irish Water Spaniels, or from a small variety of Newfoundland plus some crossing with Poodles. This would account for the tight curls from head through tail tip. Wherever it came from, the dog has proved one of the best of the duck-hunting retrievers, particularly in water. It is a tireless and avid swimmer, easy to train, affec-

Cruft's Show is the most important canine event of the year in Britain.

Curly-coated Retriever

tionate, big but not bumbling. Breed standards call for a jet-black or solid liver-colored coat. Weight ranges from 70 to 80 pounds, and average height is from 25 to 27 inches. It has achieved its greatest popularity in England, Australia, and New Zealand. (Sporting: 1–3; Gundog: 2–4)

CUSHION: a fullness of the upper lip, as in the Pekingese.

CYNOLOGIST: one who studies dogs.

DACHSBRACKE: Also known as the Drever, this dog of Swedish ancestry has never achieved the popularity of its stouter counterpart, the Basset. It is a good trailing dog with a keen nose and, as one would expect, a fine voice. Males stand 13 to 16 inches at the shoulder, females a bit less. Color is white with brown, reddish, or black patches. (Hound: 2)

Dachsbracke

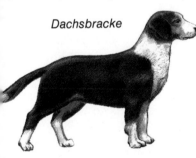

DACHSHUND: This charming little dog with the low-slung chassis has long been a favorite in many nations, both for show and as a house pet. The Dachshund is most probably of German origin, although an underslung dog depicted on the tomb of one of the Pharaohs looks suspiciously like it.

A game, alert, and lively performer, the Dachshund formerly worked creditably as an earth dog (a digger), or was utilized to track game or drive it to a sportsman's gun. It is not used widely for hunting these days except as a rat killer: powerful jaws fit the dog superbly for this chore.

The Dachshund comes in a wide variety of coats, colors, and sizes. Since breed standards differ all over the world, it is best to examine show requirements in the area where you live. In general, the varieties are as follows:

(1) Smooth or Shorthaired: Smooth, glossy, short, easy-to-groom coat, either one-color, two-color, or dappled; weight from 23 to 25 pounds.

(2) Wirehaired: Short, rough, hard thick coat. Like the shorthair, it is a close-to-the-ground dog, but can be a shade taller.

(3) Longhaired: A coat that is soft, gleaming, a bit wavy, and much like the Irish Setter's in appearance though not necessarily in color.

Smooth Dachshund

Longhaired Dachshund

Wirehaired Dachshund

(4) Miniatures: These can be smoothhaired, longhaired, or wirehaired, with weight varying from 7 to 12 pounds, and height from 7 to 8 inches. Colors are as varied for Miniatures as for their larger brethren.

Whatever its size, color, or coat, a Dachshund loves to play, can run longer on its short legs without getting tired than a human being can on much longer ones, is companionable, and is undeniably a barker if strangers approach your door. (Hound: 1–2–3–4)

DALMATIAN: Once upon a time the Dalmatian was a carriage or firehouse dog, trotting happily beneath horse-drawn vehicles; today it is most often a house pet. Its short coat is easily kept clean, and it has little or no doggy smell. In its time this extremely ancient spotted breed has served as a war dog and guard dog, sheepherder, boar hunter, and circus performer.

The Dalmatian is a fine companion and not much of a barker (exceptions are known, however). It is reserved and polite with strangers but a good guardian as well. A born runner, this big dog (19 to 24 inches at the withers, 50 to 55 pounds in weight) is strong and has vast powers of endurance. (Nonsporting: 1–3–4; Utility; 2)

Dalmatian

DAM: a female parent.

DANDIE DINMONT: Do not be deceived by its large melting eyes for this tough little character has a mind of its own and is highly opinionated. Dandie Dinmont was the name of the farmer who owned six rough-coated border dogs in *Guy Mannering*, and the character in Sir Walter Scott's novel passed his name on to the breed and made it extremely popular.

The Dandie is not a lapdog by nature, but if you are seeking a

Dandie Dinmont

pet who makes an exciting and interesting companion and who insists on equal rights, it will suit your needs perfectly. It should be 8 to 11 inches tall and weigh from 18 to 24 pounds. With soft, silky hair covering his head and a crisp body coat, the Dandie requires light grooming to appear at his best. Color should range from blue-gray to light silver or from dark ochre to cream. (Terrier: 1–2–3–4)

DANDRUFF: the result of excessive shedding of the cells from the top layer of the skin. It appears as dry flakes in the hair and may be due to inadequate diet, too frequent bathing, or disease. Proper diagnosis is essential, and not all cases (as in man) can be permanently cured.

DAPPLED: mottled markings of various colors.

DEAFNESS: inability to hear sounds. Deafness may be partial or complete, and is usually present if a dog does not respond to a whistle (high sound) or a handclap (low sound).

Some albino dogs (those that are completely white with pale noses and nails) are born deaf; therefore, all white puppies lacking eye rim, nose and lip pigment should be tested before purchase. Deaf dogs get along very well indoors, but *must* be kept on a leash outdoors, as they cannot hear automobiles or other approaching dangers. For causes of deafness, see *ear diseases*.

DEBARKING: a surgical procedure in which a portion of the vocal chords is removed. After the operation the dog is unable to make loud, high-pitched sounds.

DEERHOUND: see *Scottish deerhound*.

DENMARK: The National authority is the Dansk Kennelklub, Norrebrogade 40, DK 2200, Copenhagen.

DERBY: a field-trial contest for young dogs, most often those of one to two years old.

DEWCLAW: the first toe (the equivalent of the thumb in man) on the inside of the front legs. If present on the hind legs at birth, dewclaws are usually removed to prevent later injury. However, the AKC standard for some breeds (e.g., Briards) requires double dewclaws on both hind legs while in others it is common practice to remove both front and rear dewclaws.

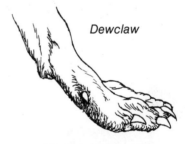

Dewclaw

DIARRHEA: the passage of soft or unformed bowel movements. Since diarrhea is a symptom of many diseases and has numerous causes, the precise treatment depends on a proper diagnosis.

Home remedy: the dog's diet should be changed and replaced with hard-boiled eggs and well-cooked rice. If diarrhea continues, consult a veterinarian.

Helpful hint: collect a specimen of stool, wrap it in aluminum foil or place in a clean container, and take it to a veterinarian for tests.

DIGESTION: the process by which foods are changed so that they can be absorbed and utilized by the body. Digestion starts in the mouth. The food is mixed with saliva, which acts as a lubricant for easy passage through the gullet (esophagus) and into the stomach. Unlike man, there are no digestive enzymes in a dog's saliva.

The food is mixed in the stomach with acids and enzymes (hydrochloric acid and pepsin), which start the breakdown of proteins and carbohydrates; it then passes through the pyloric valve to the duodenum, is mixed with bile (to digest fats) and with other enzymes. These processes continue in the small intestine until the food passes through the ileocolic valve and reaches the colon. Here water is absorbed, and the undigested portions pass into the rectum and are excreted.

Dingo

DINGO: The only true wild dog existing today, the Dingo is a resident of Australia. How or when it got there no one knows, although it is theorized that Dingoes may have been brought to that continent by tribes of aborigines thousands of years ago. Pure speci-

mens of the breed (some 22 inches tall and brown or yellowish-red) are rare, since it mates freely with domestic dogs of the region. (See also *wild dogs*.)

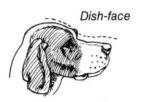

Dish-face

DISH-FACED: having the nose higher at the tip than at the top.

DISINFECTANTS: agents that kill bacteria instead of inhibiting their spread, as antiseptics do. Lye (caustic soda, or sodium hydroxide) is one of the best disinfectants known for destroying roundworm eggs and other parasites and bacteria in kennels. Dissolve two pounds of lye in 10 gallons of *cold* water and make sure to treat cracks, spaces under fences, and corners. Avoid inhaling lye dust or getting the solution on your skin or in your eyes. Lye solution can be used on concrete or bare wooden floors, but must be washed down thoroughly an hour or so after application. Wear rubber boots and gloves when treating a kennel with lye solution.

Chlorine bleaches, diluted to the strength recommended on the bottle, are effective disinfectants if the kennel area has been scrubbed first. Hose down the chlorine solution thirty minutes after you have applied it. Make sure that dogs and aluminum dishes are well away from the area you are treating. The fumes are strong, and chlorine sets up a chemical reaction with aluminum.

Cresols are less effective than lye as disinfectants, but do a good job when used as directed, and are safer to work with than lye.

DISLOCATION OF THE KNEE (OR STIFLE JOINT): a condition in which the kneecap (patella) moves out of its groove on the thighbone (femur). Such dislocation is common in Poodles, Pekingese, and other small breeds. Some cases recover spontaneously, others need corrective surgery.

DISQUALIFICATION: the decision of a judge or bench-show committee to bar a dog from further competition in a given show. Such decisions are based on any condition that makes a dog ineligible under the rules for the show or because it has a fault unacceptable in its breed standard.

DISTEMPER: Canine distemper is a very serious and often fatal disease. It is caused by a filterable *virus* similar, but not identical, to the measles virus in children.

Prevention:

(1) Immunization: Excellent vaccines are now available and can be given by several methods. In all of them the first doses should be injected as soon after weaning as possible, and the final dose between twelve and sixteen weeks of age. Older dogs can be immunized with a single dose of vaccine. Recent studies have shown that about 20 percent of dogs lose some of their immunity after one year; consequently, a booster dose is recommended annually.

(2) Sanitation: The canine-distemper virus is an extremely infectious one, and even a small number of virus particles can cause the disease in a susceptible dog. The virus is present in discharges from eyes, nose, and feces, and is carried in droplet form in the air, on clothing, and on the ground. Infected animals must be kept completely isolated and not exercised on public streets. Because the virus is present in the air, treatment of the premises with disinfectant is usually not effective, but plenty of fresh air (from open windows) will dilute the virus. The virus can also remain dormant in ice and snow, and then become active again after thawing.

The *incubation period* is from ten to fourteen days.

Symptoms vary greatly. Distemper usually starts with a fever and loss of appetite. Later there may be ocular and nasal discharges, vomiting, and diarrhea. Complications are common and include pneumonia or nerve damage (convulsions, chorea, or paralysis).

Treatment must be supervised by a veterinarian, and good nursing care is essential.

DOBERMAN PINSCHER: The Dobe was developed late in the nineteenth century by Ludwig Dobermann, a German (and the name is spelled with two *n*'s everywhere except in the United States and Canada). Originally a somewhat cloddish dog, the sleek and powerful animal of today represents patient blending of Rottweiler, German Pinscher, and, most probably, Weimaraner strains. The Doberman combines the agility of a Terrier with the strength of far larger breeds. Intel-

Doberman Pinscher

ligent and easily trainable, it is a much respected watchdog, a good hunter, and usually a devoted pet.

The Doberman ranges in height from 24 to 28 inches at the withers and weighs in the neighborhood of 45 pounds. Its smooth, short coat can be black, tan, fawn, or blue with red points. (Working: 1–2–3–4)

DOCKING: shortening of the tail. Docking should be done at three to four days of age, at which time it is an almost painless process. Most dogs are born with long tails, and docking is required for nearly all Terrier and Spaniel breeds, all Pinschers, German Shorthaired Pointers, Boxers, Old English Sheepdogs, and many others. The exact length is specified in the breed standard.

Docking a tail

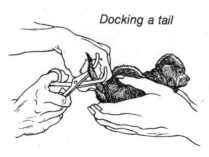

DOGNAPPING: Equivalent to kidnapping, the theft of valuable animals for resale to individuals or for research purposes has assumed formidable proportions in the United States. The best safeguards are: (1) don't permit your dog to run free except when it is being supervised; (2) when left in a car, protect your dog by locking the door and rolling the window down an inch or two for ventilation; (3) if your dog is in a fenced-in area, make sure the gate is padlocked. (See also *tattooing*.)

Dogue de Bordeaux

DOGUE DE BORDEAUX: The national watch-dog of France is one of the oldest of all breeds. Bearing a close resemblance to the Bullmastiff, it ranges up to 30 inches in height and may reach a weight of close to 150 pounds. It is shown widely in Europe and continues to be highly prized as a guardian of the home and a calm and affectionate family favorite.

DOMED SKULL: a top skull rounded like half a ball.

DOWN-FACED: having a muzzle that curves downward from the skull to the tip of the nose.

DROP EAR: see *button ear*.

Domed Skull

DRY: absence of surplus flesh around the throat, mouth, or lips.

DRY NECK: firm, unwrinkled neck skin.

DUAL CHAMPION: any dog that has earned a championship at both a bench show and a field trial.

DUDLEY NOSE: a flesh-colored nose.

Down-faced

Dudley Nose

E

EAR CROPPING: a surgical operation in which part of the earflap is removed so that the ears stand erect. It is said to improve the appearance and has no connection with a dog's health. Cropping is illegal in many countries. The operation is usually performed at six to twelve weeks of age, depending on the breed, and should always be done under general anesthesia. After surgery the ears must be supported and trained until healing is complete. Breeds commonly cropped include Boxers, Pinschers, Great Danes, Schnauzers, Bouviers, and Boston Terriers.

Cropped Ears

EAR DISEASES: Often termed cankers, ear diseases are very common in dogs. They are painful and must be treated promptly.

Symptoms: The dog will shake its head constantly. Examination with a pen-light will show redness and often a foul-smelling discharge. Sticks and powders should never be used by amateurs because the lining of the ear is very delicate and easily injured.

Causes include:

(1) Excess wax (mostly in sporting breeds and Poodles).

(2) Parasites, such as ear mites (otodectes) or fleas.

(3) Chemicals, e.g., strong shampoos and dips.

(4) Infections.

(5) Tumors.

Middle-ear conditions often follow any of the above. The eardrum is injured or ruptured, and the dog may become deaf.

Inner-ear conditions may cause dizziness or circling, and are always serious because they can spread to the brain.

Treatment depends upon the cause and needs professional diagnosis. To relieve the pain temporarily, a few drops of warm mineral oil should be dropped into the outer ear canal.

Most ear conditions can be treated or controlled medically. If such conditions do not respond to treatment, surgery is sometimes necessary.

ECZEMA: a word used loosely to describe many different diseases in which the dog's skin is itchy and inflamed. Eczema may be due to fleas, fungi, allergies, or a wide variety of other causes. A veterinarian should be consulted.

EDEMA: a condition in which the tissues of the body become filled with water. Edema may be local (due to impaired circulation) or general (due to heart and kidney diseases). Edema manifests itself as a soft doughy swelling under the skin.

ELBOW: the joint between the upper arm and forearm formed by the humerus, radius and ulna.

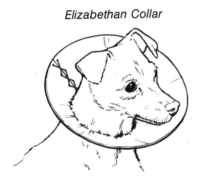

Elizabethan Collar

ELIZABETHAN COLLAR: a device, generally made of stiff cardboard, used to prevent dogs from reaching and tearing off bandages, scratching open wounds, etc. A hole the size of a dog's neck is cut in the cardboard and a slit is made from the hole to the outside edge. The collar is then fitted around the dog's neck and the open ends are stapled or taped together. (See also *bandaging*.)

ELKHOUND: see *Norwegian Elkhound*.

English Cocker Spaniel

ENGLISH COCKER SPANIEL: "Spanyells" originated centuries ago in Spain, and it is likely that the smaller puppies in a litter were trained to hunt woodcock. Hence the "cocker," as contrasted with the larger dogs, now known as Springers or Field Spaniels, who were used to spring game. Slightly larger than its American counterpart, the English Cocker has been highly popular for decades, and justifiably so, for it is fun-loving and lively by nature and beautiful to behold, thanks in no small part to its liquid eyes and silky coat. Colors range from solid black to solid white with a wide range of parti-colors in between. Dogs at the withers are about 17 inches, bitches, 15 inches; and weight ranges from 26 to 34 pounds. (Sporting: 1–3; Gundog: 2–4)

ENGLISH FOXHOUND: This big dog (23 to 25 inches at the shoulder, weight around 85 pounds) is rarely seen in the show ring or kept as a pet. It was bred solely for the hunt and can be found, in the American or English version, wherever riding to hounds remains a popular sport. At this it excels, for it has a keen nose, great drive, and vast endurance. On a chase Foxhounds will lead the horses sixty miles or more and perform

English Foxhound

perfectly; once back in the kennel it most likely will resist strenuously all attempts at domestication. (Hound: 1–2–3–4)

ENGLISH SETTER: Many centuries ago this breed's British ancestors were used to "set" birds—that is, to find and point toward them, and then crouch and "set" while the owner edged past to toss a net over their catch. Later these dogs performed the same functions when guns came into general use. The breed was brought to its present peak of beauty and proficiency by two Englishmen, Edward Laverack, who, beginning in 1825, produced generations of fine show dogs, and by R. L. Purcell Llewellin, who five decades later introduced a new strain that caused English Setters

English Setter

to sweep top show and field-trial honors.

Its beauty, combined with intelligence and a sweet disposition, has enabled the English Setter to retain much of its popularity. Size ranges from 24 to 26 inches at the withers, with bitches not below 22 inches; weight is 55 to 65 pounds.

English Setters are varicolored, but animals that are flecked all over are preferred to those with large patches of a single shade. (Sporting: 1–3; Gundog: 2–4)

English Springer Spaniel

ENGLISH SPRINGER SPANIEL: The perfect hunting dog for a man who wants to go out with his gun and one dog, this oldest of the Spaniel breeds remains nearly as popular today with specialists as it was four hundred years ago. Its trainability and intelligence, ability to cover ground rapidly, medium size, and compact body have kept this handsome dog a favorite among hunters and field-trial enthusiasts. Like all of its relatives, the English Springer is a good family pet.

Usually liver and white or black and white, an adult dog is 19 to 20 inches tall at the withers and weighs from 49 to 55 pounds; bitches are slightly smaller. (Sporting: 1–3; Gundog: 2–4)

ENGLISH TOY SPANIEL: One cannot find these little dogs under that name in England, where they are listed as Cavalier King Charles or King Charles Spaniels. In the United States and Canada they are generally shown in two classes, Blenheim and Prince Charles and, in the second group, King Charles and Ruby. In any event, these silky-coated gentle little dogs (weight 9 to 12 pounds) still have hunting blood in their veins. (Toy: 1–3)

English Toy Terrier

ENGLISH TOY TERRIER: Presently known in the New World as *Toy Manchester Terriers*, the breed has had many other confusing aliases (*Black and Tan, Toy Black and Tan, Miniature Black and Tan,* etc.) over the years. They have true terrier instincts, are high-spirited and alert and were once adept rat killers. In the United Kingdom standards call for weight ranging from 6 to 8 pounds and shoulder height of 10 to 12 inches. In the United States the weight may not exceed 12 pounds: (Toy: 2–4 and, under the name Toy Manchester Terrier: 1–3.)

ENTERITIS: inflammation of the small intestine, which may be due to worms, bacteria, viruses, or bad food. Enteritis usually causes diarrhea, and treatment depends on the cause.

ENVIRONMENTAL FEAR: Some puppies, at four to five months of age, show fear when in an unfamiliar place or situation. Generally this disappears as the dog reaches adulthood, but if anything highly unpleasant or unsettling occurs at this time—a thunderstorm, for example—there is a danger that the momentary unease may develop into a phobia that requires care and great patience to overcome.

EPILEPSY: a brain disease characterized by periodic convulsions. The dog may or may not lose consciousness. After an attack, it may become disoriented and wander aimlessly, or may lapse into deep sleep if not disturbed. Very little is known about the cause of epilepsy in dogs or man. Most cases are incurable, but many can be controlled with some of the newer drugs. Emergency treatment aims at restraint of the dog to prevent damage to itself or the family.

Note: Not all convulsions are due to epilepsy. They may also be caused by tumors, worms, hysteria, or viruses (see *distemper*). Some forms of epilepsy are thought to be congenital in various strains of certain breeds.

ESKIMO DOG: These rugged Arctic dogs can pull huge loads through heavy snow over incredible distances. Magnificent work animals, they somehow acquired a reputation for viciousness and bad temper. Actually, any such

Eskimo Dogs pull a heavy load across an Arctic wasteland.

characteristics stem from the fact that most of the animals are kept out of doors and rarely experience human companionship. An Eskimo pup raised as part of a human family will prove as gentle and rewarding a pet as any other breed. Weight, 50 to 85 pounds, depending on sex. (Working: 3)

ESP: Some students of the dog claim that it has a "six sense" which amounts to a form of extrasensory perception. To prove their point they cite cases, some rather well documented, of pets who have made long journeys (across large bodies of water, in some situations) to find owners who had traveled several hundred miles away. While there is no scientific proof to buttress the claims of ESP in dogs, there is no doubt that they do communicate with one another wordlessly, using their own form of body language. They solicit play by a raised paw or a half-crouch; show aggression by bared teeth and raised hair; submission by rolling over; happiness by a wagging tail, and fear or unhappiness by the same tail tucked woefully between the hind legs. Thus, it is not beyond the realm of possibility that they may go far beyond these elementary examples of body language, in ways we do not know about or understand.

EUTHANASIA: an easy and painless death (according to Webster). Accepted methods include an overdose of anesthetic agents by injection or inhalation, or a decompression air chamber. Euthanasia is recommended for all animals suffering from incurable, painful diseases.

From a cave rock painting found in Tessili-n-Ajjer.

EVOLUTION AND HISTORY OF THE DOG: While the direct ancestors of the dog are unknown, most paleontologists believe that its remote forbears shared the earth's surface with dinosaurs in the Cretaceous period. They were called creodonts, and were most likely mouse-sized mammals whose teeth were sharp enough, and tiny brains shrewd enough, to enable them to survive in a world that proved to be too much for the massive reptiles.

Scientists are uncertain as to whether a minklike animal called *Miacis*, who lived some 40 million years ago, or a later mammal known as *Daphocnodon* or *Cynodictis* (a mere 20 million years back) was a progenitor of the *Canidae* of today. We do know that both of these mammals, who lived millions of years before history began, closely resembled the civet cat, a foxlike animal whose anal glands secrete a fluid that is the basis for much of the world's perfume.

In any event, from *Cynodictis*, and a later descendant known as *Cynodesmus*, came *Tomarctus*, an extremely doglike animal from whose family tree came all of the *canids*—jackals and wolves, foxes and the domesticated dog.

To this statement it should be added that a link is still missing between Tomarctus and today's dog. It is genetically impossible for foxes and dogs to mate and have fertile offspring. Hyenas and jackals have been mentioned as possible forebears, but their characteristics are too different to make this a possibility. Wolves and dogs

The ancestor of all present day dogs is thought to be the Tomarctus that lived about 15 million years ago.

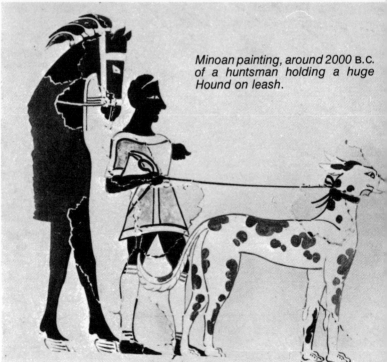

Minoan painting, around 2000 B.C. of a huntsman holding a huge Hound on leash.

Egyptian wall painting (circa 1450 B.C.) of a Hound pack in action.

could be crossbred and produce fertile litters, and this possibility is perhaps the basis for the centuries' old tales of such crossbreeding. However, since recorded history, adult wolves and dogs have killed each other, if they could, and have shown no interest in sex. It is more likely that accounts of wolf-dog matings are really stories of the unions of wild (feral) dogs with domestic dogs. These recognize one another readily, and if one gives the "I surrender" signal (by rolling over on its back with its feet in the air), the other stops attacking at once. Wolves and dogs may be first cousins, but the true immediate ancestor of the dog has yet to be found. Fossils of small canids in northern Asia may hold the key, but archaeologists have not yet unearthed definitive evidence.

Assyrian wall sculpture depicts a hunting Mastiff with what appears to be a modern choke-collar.

81

THE DOG IN HISTORY

This lamblike dog is a magnificent example of Chinese ceramics from the T'ang Dynasty, around 700 A.D.

We first encounter the dog as a domesticated animal in rock paintings dating back some 12,000 years. Almost always the dog is depicted as a Paleolithic hunter, pursuing deer or antelope or far larger prey, with or without his owner. From these marvelous drawings found in caves it becomes quite clear that primitive man did not regard the dog as a source of food but rather as a companion in the search for sustenance, a creature with whom peaceful coexistence was highly desirable.

Nearly 2,000 years after the eruption of Mt. Vesuvius, archaeologists unearthed this perfectly preserved and calcified dog in the ruins of Pompeii.

Stark Roman realism is almost overwhelming in this statue of an unhappy Diogenes and his lonely looking little dog.

In other parts of the world, however, dogs began to act as shepherds and guardians of domestic cattle, a role they have filled admirably to this day.

By the beginning of the Christian era the dog had become almost completely modernized. That is to say, he had become a house pet and hunter, a racing machine and protector of the home, a vermin killer and palace favorite, a circus performer and prize-fighter. His use as a guide for the blind and messenger in war alone remained to be developed.

83

Dog (a Great Dane?). Detail from The Hunt of the Unicorn, *a tapestry, probably Flemish, about 1500.*

"A public duel between a dog and the gentleman who killed his master," reads the rather astonishing legend on this 14th Century engraving.

LE COMBAT D'UN CHIEN CONTRE UN GENTILHOMME
QUI AVOIT TUÉ SON MAISTRE FAICT A MONTARGIS.
Soubs le regne de Charles V. en 1371.

A portion of Breughel's Winter Landscape *shows hunters with at least five different breeds.*

British aristocrats often had their portraits painted with a dog somewhere in the picture. Gainsborough's The Morning Walk *(1785) is a good example.*

85

Mary Cassatt's Woman With a Dog, *a impressionistic portrait of a Terrier who looks as though he wanted to bound off in pursuit of something.*

While many breeds have remained virtually unchanged in appearance over the centuries, the majority have altered greatly in appearance as they have been bred to improve one or another physical quality. Some are bigger than their ancestors, some smaller; some are leggier, some are leaner; some have heavier coats, some are smoother. All of these processes of change will continue in the future, but basically the dog will continue to be what he has been for so many millenia—a faithful friend and companion of man.

Pluto, Walt Disney's disreputable hound, became famous the world over.

©Walt Disney Productions

Landseer's painting of two very comfortable companions.

Few owners have the space to give their animals the sort of exercise these English Setters are so enjoying.

EXERCISE: Aside from stating that dogs which are rarely exercised become bored and tend to get into mischief, it is difficult to go beyond generalizations on this subject. Here are a few of them: (1) most, but not all, big dogs need more exercise than small ones; (2) Hounds and sporting breeds generally prefer a vigorous outdoor life more than working dogs, Terriers, or Toys, but this is not true of all of them; (3) all dogs should be given a change of scenery several times each day, but here again, some city dwellers with paper-trained animals rarely if ever exercise their animals, and neither dog nor owner appears unhappy with the results; (4) dogs who are left alone a good part of the time definitely need to get out in the world on a regular basis.

For city dwellers who are contemplating buying a dog, here are several additional injunctions. Assuming you do not belong to the school that plans to paper-train an animal and keep it indoors (the larger the dog the more unesthetic this practice becomes), remember that all days are not clement and that you must be prepared to go outdoors in rain, snow, sleet, or smog. No matter how earnestly children promise to exercise a dog, one must realize that many of them backslide after a few weeks or months and leave the job to the adults in the family. Big dogs seem even bigger in small apartments.

Finally, there is the growing environmental problem of excrement on city streets and sidewalks. Good manners impose on all owners an obligation to make certain that dogs relieve themselves in streets rather than on pavements,

The "Let's-get-into-mischief" look

but even this may not solve the pollution problem in the near future. More and more communities are discussing the passage of laws that will heavily penalize owners who do not clean up after their dogs. Even if such legislation is not enacted, true ecologists will carry with them a metal scooper and a plastic bag inside a larger paper bag, the contents of which can be flushed away once they are back home.

The "oops-sorry" look

The "what-can-that-be" look

The "something's-going-to-happen" look

EXPRESSION: the front view of the features of a dog's head, particulary the set and shape of the eyes.

By their facial expressions dogs, and notably puppies, manage to convey virtually all emotions—joy, dejection, expectation, fear, anger and many more

EXTINCT BREEDS: in a sense the term is a misnomer, for breeds change in conformation and habits over the centuries rather than pass out of existence completely. Crossbreeding and inbreeding have added to, or subtracted from, the height, weight, or other physical characteristics, a process which with the passage of years

The "please-don't-leave-me" look

has led to the disappearance from the scene of scores, perhaps hundreds, of once popular breeds. Nonetheless, the Basset Hound or the Golden Retriever, the Afghan or the German Shepherd of 1974 bears a startling resemblance to his long forgotten ancestors. A few vanished, or almost-forgotten breeds are shown below.

Russian Tracker

Canis Familiaris

Molossian Dog

Alaunt

Shock Dog

Talhund

Alano

Sleuth Hound

Braque

Brabanter

EYE DISEASES AND INJURIES:
A dog with a diseased eye will show one or more of the following symptoms: discharge, pain on looking into light, or rubbing its paw over the eye. If the condition is due to an injury or occurs suddenly, the dog should be taken to a veterinarian immediately, since an apparently minor situation may become complicated if not treated correctly. As a first-aid measure the owner may flush the eye with a solution of a half-teaspoon of table salt in one pint of warm boiled water.

Common diseases of the eyelids include:

(1) Entropion, in which the lids roll inward and irritate the sensitive cornea.

(2) Ectropion, in which the lids turn outward (as seen in Saint Bernards) and expose the cornea to dust and wind.

(3) Distriasis, or the presence of small hairs at the lid margins, which turn in and irritate the cornea. These three conditions are usually treated surgically.

(4) The harderian gland is a small structure on the inside of the nictitating membrane (the third eyelid, or haw). If dislocated, the gland appears as a round red pea on the inner (nasal) side of the eye. This condition is not painful and the gland can be removed surgically without any change in the dog's appearance.

Diseases of the eye itself include:

(1) Conjunctivitis

(2) Corneal ulcers

(3) Cataracts

(4) Glaucoma

(5) Progressive retinal atrophy (night blindness). This is a serious degeneration of the retina leading to blindness. It has been recognized in Irish Setters, Collies, Retrievers, Poodles, and many other breeds. The disease is considered to be hereditary, but may not appear until the dog is three to four years old. In order to eradicate the condition, responsible breeders have the eyes of their breeding stock examined by a veterinary ophthamologist and receive certification if their animals are found free of the disease.

EYETEETH: the upper canines.

Pyrame

Talbott Hound

St. Huber Hound

F

FAKING: altering an animal's appearance to conceal a fault. A dog whose appearance has been artificially altered is automatically barred from competition.

FALL: hair hanging over the face.

FALSE PREGNANCY (*Pseudocyesis*): a condition in the bitch that simulates true pregnancy, although no puppies are present in the uterus. It usually occurs eight to eleven weeks after heat. The bitch is restless, may make a nest, usually has milk in her breasts, and gives other signs of imminent parturition. Mild cases subside spontaneously, but if severe or prolonged, medical treatment is necessary. The cause is probably a disturbance of the hormone balance of the ovaries.

F.C.I.: the Fédération Cynologique Internationale, an organization founded in 1911 to promote the exchange of information and standardization of canine procedures among nations. Twenty-four countries in Europe, Africa, Central and South America belong to the Federation while a dozen others, the United Kingdom and the Republic of South Africa among them, have reciprocal agreements with the F.C.I. concerned with the passage of information. The United States, Canada and Australia are not members.

While the F.C.I. is primarily concerned with mutual agreement on such matters as stud books, breed standards and disciplinary measures regarding judges and officials, it also controls dog shows and working trials at which two important degrees are eagerly sought: C.A.C.I.T., an International Working Trial Championship and C.A.C.I.B., an International Beauty Championship.

FEAR BITING: see *shyness*.

Feathering

FEATHERING: a fringe of hair on the ears, body, legs, or tail that is longer than the coat on the rest of the body.

FETCH: a command to bring an object to one, or, in the field, to retrieve game.

FIDDLE FRONT: a condition in which the front legs are out at elbows, the pasterns (or the part of the foot between the wrist and toes) are close, and the feet are turned out. Also called "French front."

Field Spaniel

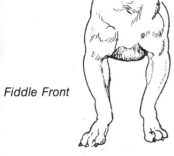
Fiddle Front

organizations. In Great Britain the title is *F.T. Ch.* and goes to dogs that have won a specified number of open stakes.

FIELD SPANIEL: Rarest of all the Spaniel breeds, the Field Spaniel's relative lack of popularity probably results from the fact that in the nineteenth century breeders managed to produce a genuinely ugly Spaniel, with an exaggerated long body, short legs, a heavy head, and so much bone that the dog moved with difficulty. Crosses between Springers and Cockers have improved the breed. Today the dog (averaging 18 inches high at the shoulder and weighing from 35 to 50 pounds) is much better balanced, has reasonable speed

FIELD CHAMPION: The title of field champion is awarded to dogs that have defeated a specified number of competitors at a series of field trials licensed by the American Kennel Club or by member

American Field Trial Champion, Saighton's Saul (front center), flanked by three kennelmates.

A Pointer and a Setter take off eagerly after their quarry in a field trial held in Pinehurst, North Carolina.

and agility, and possesses plenty of endurance. While the coat is generally black, it can vary widely. Abundant feathering is a breed characteristic. (Sporting: 1–3; Gundog: 2–4)

FIELD TRIALS—AMERICAN: Nearly six thousand field trials, ranging from highly formalized championship events down to unsanctioned and unrecorded trials, are held annually in the United States, making this form of competition the most popular of all canine activities. More than four thousand trials are licensed by the American Kennel and United Kennel clubs with separate events held for different breeds. The "quarry" varies widely—from live foxes, raccoons, rabbits, hares, pheasants, and ducks to dead or "planted" birds, dummies, or even bottled scents. In the case of daytime coon chases the trail is often laid by dragging a bag containing raccoon feces across the course.

Most of the championship trials are grueling tests of skill and endurance. American Foxhound trials, which in the South attract up to five hundred entries, last as long as five days. At nighttime Coonhound trials, dogs and owners fight through tangled woodlands and swamps to find and "tree" wild raccoons. Beagles, working singly, in braces, or packs, participate by the hundreds in chasing rabbits or hare. Other, somewhat smaller trials are held for Dachshunds, Bassets, Pointers, Setters, and Retrievers. Of the Spaniels only Brittany and English Spaniels compete nowadays, virtually all the others having been retired to less arduous avocations. Many trials have attendance figures running into the thousands. Betting on the results is often heavy, and up to $40,000 in prize money has been paid out at a single coon chase.

FIELD TRIALS—BRITISH: Unlike American trials, there is nothing artificial about gundog competition in the British Isles. Trials last a day, and strict rules specify that every aspect must conform to what might be expected to happen if a man and a dog went out on their own. Trials for different breeds stress only what a specific breed is supposed to do best. Thus, a Setter is tested on quartering the ground, detecting quarry by scent, and leading the hunter up to a bird without flushing it.

Trials in Great Britain are held in the appropriate season for Setters, Pointers, Retrievers, and, unlike the United States, a variety of Spaniels. The number of entries generally ranges from ten to twenty-four, with most trials divided into three classes—Puppy, Novice, and Open. No field trials are held for Hounds. To become a champion, a dog must win a specified number of open stakes.

One interesting anomaly in British trials is that Pointer-Retriever breeds, such as the German Shorthaired Pointer, are supposed to retrieve as well as point. As a result they are ineligible for both Pointer *and* Retriever trials and must compete among themselves.

In all countries individuals wishing to enter their dogs in field trials should consult local kennel clubs for information regarding time, place, and entry specifications.

Sending out a contestant to retrieve the prey in an English Field Trial.

FIGHTS AND FIGHTERS: Most dogs are amiable characters who have a considerable degree of phoniness in their make-up. Separated by a fence or other unbridgeable barrier, they bark and snarl furiously at one another. When two males on leads meet, they are likely to stalk menacingly around each other, growling (or cursing, if you will) softly. If one owner tugs at the lead, a fight may well ensue, but if both owners permit the leads to remain loose, it is more than likely that a few reassuring sniffs will cause both animals to relax and, often, start playing with one another. If a fight looks imminent, however, the dogs should be pulled apart by both owners with sharp jerks on the leads. A smart slap on the hindquarters often works as well.

In the event a fight develops, here are some points to keep in mind:

(1) Attempts at separating dogs physically often make them fight more fiercely.

(2) Left to their own devices, one dog or the other will often beat a retreat.

(3) Efforts to pull one dog away from another often ends with the arbitrator getting bitten or badly scratched and with unnecessary injury to the weaker dog.

On the other hand, once a dog sinks its teeth into an adversary's flesh, interference is essential. Of the many suggested methods of breaking such a hold—a pail of water or the spray of a water hose in the aggressor's face, ammonia on a cloth or broom, a lighted match or cigarette applied to the male's testicles or to the inside flank of a bitch—one may work.

To break dogs who are compulsive fighters of the habit, two somewhat draconian measures may possibly bring results: (1) purchase a prod, which will send a sharp electric jolt through the animal's system; (2) douse the dog with a spray of chemical Mace, which causes acute eye pain but does no permanent damage.

Finally, dogs who persist in attacking other dogs and cannot be broken of the habit should either be confined or disposed of.

FILA BRASILEIRE: A recognized Brazilian breed, this is a Mastiff-type dog used for guarding, tracking, and herding. It was most probably introduced into Central America by the Conquistadores and had its origin in Spain.

FINLAND: The recognized canine authority is Suomen Kennelliitto —Finska Kennelklubben, Bulevardi 14a, Helisinki 12.

FINNISH SPITZ: One of the oldest of all breeds, the Spitz is little known beyond the land from which it takes its name. A hunting hound, the Spitz tracked furred animals in earlier days, from bears down to

Finnish Spitz

rabbits, but in our time it has been used to hunt grouse and other birds. During recent decades efforts have been made in Finland and England to restore the breed, which lost much of its identity and working qualities through endless crossings with other Scandinavian breeds. Although these resulted in a dog with many fine qualities, registrations in England, where it is officially recognized, are still low. Size ranges from 17½ to 20 inches for dogs, from 15½ to 18 inches for bitches. The thick coat is reddish-brown or on the yellow side. (Hound: 2)

Flat-coated Retriever

FLAT-COATED RETRIEVER: Formerly called the "Wavy-Coated Retriever" this medium-size gun-dog (height from 22 to 23 inches at the withers for dogs, weight from 50 to 70 pounds) made its appearance in England a bit more than a century ago. Originally, the Flat-Coat aroused considerable interest among breeders, but during recent decades it has been eclipsed by the more popular Labradors and Goldens, despite the fact that it shares all of their good qualities as a swimmer, retriever and house pet. Its dense coat is black or liver-colored. (Sporting: 1–3; Gundog: 2)

FLATULENCE: the build-up of gas in the colon and its elimination through the rectum. It may be caused by eating gassy foods, beans or leafy vegetables, or rich organ meats or by insufficient exercise. Owners can reduce flatulence by correcting the diet and by providing more adequate exercise.

FLEAS: small wingless insects with long legs. Dog fleas prefer to live on the dog, but if hungry will attack cats or people.

Symptoms include itching and scratching. The adult flea is easily seen as a small brown creature moving rapidly through the hair of the back and hindquarters. The larvae appear as yellowish white flakes. Tiny black particles (the excrement of the flea) are often found throughout the hair and are always a clue to the presence of fleas.

Control of fleas must include treatment of the dog and also of its environment. Adult fleas live and feed on the dog, but they can also survive without food for more than six months in kennels, rugs, or furniture. The eggs are laid on or off the dogs, go through several metamorphoses, and, according to temperature and humidity, become mature in anywhere from eighteen days to more than a year.

Flea

Treatment of the dog: Many good commercial dips and sprays are available. They are all potential poisons, and therefore the manufacturers' directions must be read and carefully followed. Collars containing chemicals are also effective, but when they become wet they are capable of causing allergic skin reactions. Medallions are safer, but must also be used with care.

Treatment of premises: Most commercially available fly sprays will kill adult fleas. Immature forms can be removed from floors, rugs, and furniture with a vacuum cleaner. The contents of the bag must be burned in order to interrupt the fleas' life cycle. In kennels or anywhere fleas become a problem, it is advisable to repeat this procedure every two weeks.

Complications of flea infections include skin diseases and loss of weight. Fleas are also carriers of the tapeworm *dipylidium caninum*.

FLEWS: pendulous upper lips, notably at the inner corners.

FLIES: Common houseflies do not bother dogs to any extent, but stable or horse flies, which make periodic appearances in large numbers, do. They usually attack the dog's tender ears, and when the dog scratches the ears an open wound develops that in turn draws more flies. The best defense is to keep the dog in a screened area when an infestation of big flies takes place. Insect sprays do not appear to be very effective as a defensive measure although preparations used on horses do help control this problem when wiped on the tips of the dog's ears.

FLUSH: to force a bird from cover.

FLYING EARS: erect ears on a breed whose standard calls for them to be semiprick or folded.

FOOD AND NUTRITION: Few dogs are fussy eaters. A pan of water and the same diet each day of the year is completely acceptable in almost all cases. One meal a day, at a time most convenient to the owner, usually suffices for an adult dog, and if your dog walks away leaving part of the food uneaten, pick up the dish at once and reduce the quantity offered the next day. If, as more often happens, your dog wolfs down his food and pleads for more, resist this Oliver Twist appeal, since a lean animal will be happier and live longer than a fat one. A good rule of thumb in judging the right quantity of food is one-quarter to one-half ounce of food per day for each pound of body weight. Thus, a twenty-pound animal might get five to ten ounces per day—around one-half pound would be a reasonable average.

Every grocery shop and supermarket offers a wide variety of canned and packaged dog foods, almost all of which contain the carbohydrates, fats, proteins, minerals, and vitamins a dog needs. Choosing a dry food or moist canned food is up to you, although you may pay a bit extra for the water in the moist variety. There are, of course, other alternatives. A local butcher will probably sell you beef and lamb scraps at very low cost, not in itself a complete diet. Many breeders alternate raw beef chunks with kibbled biscuit (dry) or meal.

A nursing bitch needs supplements added to her diet.

A puppy, on the other hand, needs to be fed three to four times daily, and should get one-half to one ounce of food per pound of body weight each day, or double the ration of an adult dog. Its diet can also include, in addition to meat and meal, eggs, milk in moderation, and cottage cheese. At five to six months of age, a puppy should be fed twice a day. As a dog begins to approach adulthood (from seven to ten months for small breeds; later for large breeds), its nutrient needs begin to decrease gradually, and its quantity intake must be decreased to keep it trim and healthy.

Some breeders feel that bitches who are to be mated should have their diets increased slightly when they go into heat. After mating, they should be returned to normal diets, which should then be increased only as body weight increases. About a month before the litter is due, a bitch's body weight is no longer an accurate index of her nutritional needs, but she will be eating from 25 to 50 per cent more than when she is not carrying a litter.

Dogs who are sick or very old may require special foods or have the entire diet prescribed by a veterinarian.

A mother Basset and her nine pups at tea-time. They were born, appropriately enough, in Hounslow.

Most pups (but not this one) are willing to share.

A foster-mother happily adopts a kitten.

FOSTER MOTHER: a lactating bitch used to raise puppies from another bitch. Breeders need a foster mother to:

(1) Raise unusually large litters of valuable puppies.

(2) Raise the pups if the real mother has no milk or is sick or dies.

In an emergency a maternal mother cat can nurse and take care of small-breed puppies.

FOXHOUNDS: see *American, English Foxhounds*.

Three-month old pups are usually members of the clean-plate club...

101

Wirehaired Fox Terrier

Smooth Fox Terrier

FOX TERRIER: Once classified as a hunting dog for its keen vision and proficiency in routing foxes out of their holes, this gay little dog has won the hearts of its owners on every continent. There are three types:

(1) Smooth: Oldest of the trio and never a fashion-plate type of dog, the "smooth" had a humble calling—killing rats in the stables of its owners. It grew in popularity during the nineteenth century and was a consistent winner in shows on both sides of the Atlantic. Nowadays it has been largely overshadowed by its dramatic relative, the Wirehair, but it nonetheless remains a brave, wise, and good companion. The coat should be predominantly white, smooth, and hard. A dog should be not more than 15½ inches at the withers and weigh about 18 pounds; bitches should be slightly less.

(2) Wirehaired: Crossbreeding with (almost certainly) Old English rough Terriers gave the Wirehaired Fox Terrier its stiff, wiry coat. Fifty years ago it became the most popular of all breeds and remained near the top for a decade or more. It is an enormously energetic little animal with a mind of its own (some call this stubborn-

ness), a dedicated retriever of thrown rubber balls, and a way of walking that is midway between a prance and a dance. Except for its coat, breed standards are similar to those of the smooth.

(3) Toy: Bred in America, these tiny dogs (not more than 7 pounds and often half that) have smooth coats, erect ears, and docked tails held high. They have never gained recognition as a separate breed except through the National Toy Fox Terrier Association, established in the United States by the United Kennel Club. (Terriers: 1–2–3–4)

FRACTURE: a break in the continuity of the bone.

Symptoms: Following an injury, there will be a sudden onset of deformity, pain, and swelling in the affected area. Positive diagnosis is confirmed by x-rays.

First Aid: If a fracture is suspected, the dog must be kept as immobile as possible to prevent further injury. It should be placed on a flat board and taken immediately to a veterinarian. There are three main types of fractures:

(1) Simple: the bone is broken, but there is very little injury to other tissues in the area.

(2) Compound: the skin or mus-

cle around the bone is injured, and the bone may penetrate through the skin and be exposed to the air. Infection is very common in this condition.

(3) Greenstick: seen only in young dogs. The bone is broken, but the periosteum (an envelope covering the bone) is soft and elastic and is able to bend under the animal's weight. This type of fracture may cause very little pain or lameness, but if not diagnosed and treated promptly, it will heal out of line and leave a permanent deformity in the bone.

FRANCE: The principal authority in French dogdom bears the overwhelming title of Société Centrale Canine pour l'Amelioration des Races des Chiens en France, although the first three words will get a letter to its destination.

Breeds are divided into four classes: (1) Guard, Utility, and Working dogs. (2) Hunting dogs. (3) Pointing dogs. (4) Companion or "pleasure" dogs. Out of these divisions have come many of our most popular breeds, among them Bassets and Brittany Spaniels, while others—Briards, Great Pyrenees and the Bichon Frise—are coming up fast. Address: Rue de Choiseul 3F-75, Paris, 2e.

FRENCH BULLDOG: This breed isn't French at all, but is most probably the descendant of Toy English bulldogs sent across the Channel more than a century ago. Superficially, it looks like a smaller version of the English Bulldog, but there are two distinguishing exceptions:

the dog has bat ears, as opposed to the English dog's rose ears; and the skull is somewhat domed, which gives it a cheerful and ready-for-fun-and-games expression, as opposed to the dour and woe-is-me look of the British Bulldog.

French Bulldogs make fine pets and are loyal and affectionate, but for some obscure reason they do not rate high in popularity. In Great Britain, dogs weigh about 28 pounds, bitches 24. In the United States there are two classes: one for dogs under 22 pounds and another for dogs over that weight but not above 28 pounds. The coat may be white, brindle, or fawn, or brindle and white. (Nonsporting: 1–3; Utility: 2–4)

FURROW: a middle line or slight indentation from the center of the skull to the top.

FUTURITY STAKE: a show or field-trial class for young dogs nominated for entry in the event at or before birth.

French Bulldog

GAGGING: may be caused by an obstruction in the throat, tonsillitis, or other diseases.

GAIT: the way in which a dog runs or walks.

GASSY: showing an aggressive spirit.

GASTRITIS: inflammation of the lining of the stomach, which may be caused by infections, bad food, or the ingestion of irritating materials or foreign bodies. It is one cause of vomiting and occasionally can progress to the formation of an ulcer.

GASTROENTERITIS: inflammation of the stomach and small intestines, which may be acute or chronic.

Symptoms: diarrhea with or without vomiting. If severe, rapid dehydration may result.

Causes: bacteria, virus (canine distemper), parasites (hookworms or coccidia), or metallic poisons. It may also be a complication of many other diseases.

Treatment: depends on veterinarian's diagnosis of the cause.

GAY TAIL: a tail that is carried high over the back (in some breeds, this is a fault).

GERMAN SHEPHERD: A born working dog, this breed traces its

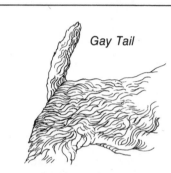

Gay Tail

antecedents to the herding and farm dogs of Germany. It became popular outside of its native land about the time of the First World War and now ranks second in popularity in the United States among AKC registered dogs and first in Great Britain, where it is known as the "Alsatian." Courageous, loyal, even-tempered, highly trainable, and keen-nosed, these

German Shepherd or Alsatian

dogs adapt as readily to being children's pets as to acting as eyes for the blind. They are cool to strangers and make excellent guard and police dogs. Exercise is a must. For show purposes, almost any color except white is permissible, though strong, dark colors are preferred. Height ranges from 22 to 26 inches at the tip of the shoulder blades; weight ranges from 60 to 85 pounds. (Working: 1–2–3–4)

*German
Shorthaired Pointer*

GERMAN SHORTHAIRED POINTER: Development of this breed began in the late nineteenth century among sportsmen who were looking for an all-purpose hunting dog. The base stock was old German Hounds that were crossbred to Spanish Pointers, English Foxhounds, and Bloodhounds. The original German Pointer was a rather cumbersome, slow dog. New bloodlines made the dog smaller and faster, but retained the character, superb nose, and endurance of the earlier type. The breed is especially popular with those who want a dog that stays close to the gun.

Their close, tight coats make them indifferent to foul weather and icy water on duck retrieves. Faithful companions, the Shorthair (21 to 25 inches at the withers; 45 to 70 pounds) is happiest outdoors. In the show ring dogs must have solid liver, liver and white, or liver-roan coat colors. (Sporting: 1–3; Gundog:2–4)

GERMAN WIREHAIRED POINTER: Virtually the counterpart of the German Shorthaired Pointer, except for its coat, which must be harsh and wiry, this breed is a fine all-around hunting dog, which works equally well with game birds, rabbits, foxes, or boars. Like the Shorthair, it is a field and not a city dog; it also reserves the bulk of its affection for one master, although it is polite to the rest of the family. Permissible coat colors are much like those of the German Shorthaired Pointer, though the head should be brown, sometimes with a white blaze. (Sporting: 1–3; Gundog: 2)

*German
Wirehaired Pointer*

GERMANY: Only West Germany has a centralized canine authority. It is called Verband für das Deutsche Hundewesen, and the address is Schwanenstrasse 30, D-46, Dortmund. Perhaps more popular breeds have evolved in

Germany than any other land save the British Isles. German breeds range from the Dachshund and Weimaraner to the Schnauzer and German Shepherd.

GESTATION: a bitch's pregnancy, which customarily lasts sixty-three days, though healthy puppies can be born any time after the fifty-eighth day. A veterinarian can make a positive diagnosis of pregnancy about seven weeks after the bitch has been mated.

GIANT SCHNAUZER: The largest of three distinct breeds of Schnauzer, the Giant Schnauzer was developed in the kingdoms of Bavaria and Württemberg by various crosses of the Standard Schnauzer with local cattle droverdogs and, at some point, with Great Danes. A high spirited, yet dependable working dog, the Giant Schnauzer's primary duties shifted from that of cattle drover and ratter to serving as a guard dog in Munich breweries and stockyards. Not really known outside Bavaria until after World War I, he became recognized as a bold and courageous military and police dog.

A large, ruggedly built, Terrier-like dog, who is intelligent, easily trained, and devoted to his family, the Giant Schnauzer is an alert, responsive companion. Breed height is specified as 25½ to 27½ inches for males; 23½ to 25½ inches for bitches. The weather resistant, dense double coat with a wiry outer coat and soft undercoat may be a salt and pepper color or solid black. The thick beard formed by heavy, blunt whiskers and the pronounced

Giant Schnauzer

arched eyebrows are distinctive features of the Schnauzer breeds. (Working: 1–3; Utility: 2, Non-sporting: 4)

Glen of Imaal Terrier

GLEN OF IMAAL TERRIER: This breed's name comes from a region in County Wicklow, Ireland, where it has existed for generations. It has become known outside Ireland recently and is beginning to make show appearances in England. A working Terrier, it is used to go to ground after such animals as badgers. In the past these dogs were pitted against one another in open fields. Although dog fighting has been illegal for more than a century, it is still required that a dog be tested in going to ground and attacking before it can attain the rank of champion.

For show ring purposes, a "natural" look is mandatory for the breed. The dog's soft, moderately long coat (wheaten, brindle, blue, or blue-tan) must not be barbered. Fourteen inches at the shoulder is considered proper height; weight should not exceed 31 pounds. (Terrier: 2)

Golden Retriever

GOLDEN RETRIEVER: As a gundog, candidate for honors in the obedience ring, and house pet who adores the entire family, the Golden Retriever rates at or near the top. It is a beautiful animal, desperately eager to please, alert and attentive to commands. Its ancestry dates back to 1865, when Lord Tweedmouth of Scotland bred the one yellow pup in a litter of black Wavy-Coated Retrievers to a liver-colored Tweed Water Spaniel. Generations of breeding produced an alert and hard-working animal possessed of a dense, water-repellent wavy or nearly straight coat in varying shades of gold. Goldens range from 20 to 24 inches in height and weigh from 55 to 70 pounds. In recent years the dependability of the breed has caused Goldens to be used as guide dogs for the blind. (Sporting: 1–3; Gundog: 2–4)

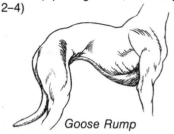

Goose Rump

GOOSE RUMP: a croup too steep or sloping.

GORDON SETTER: Named after the fourth Duke of Gordon, who gave a great deal of time and energy to perfecting an old Scottish breed at the close of the eighteenth century, this beautiful black-and-tan dog has brains and a keen nose for birds, a quiet, gentle disposition, and limitless staying power. It lacks the speed of other Setters, but is equally at home as a family companion or a gundog for those who have the facilities to exercise it. The dog's coat is soft, silky, shining coal black with tan, chestnut, or mahogany-red markings, and ideally is straight or slightly wavy.

Gordon Setter

There is considerable latitude in the breed's weight range—from 45 to 80 pounds. Height at the shoulder is from 23 to 27 inches. (Sporting: 1–3; Gundog: 2–4)

GRASS EATING: may be normal, especially in the spring, or may be a sign of indigestion or nutritional deficiency. In many dogs, grass passes through the intestinal tract undigested, but causes no problems. In others, the grass is vomited. There is no evidence to prove or disprove the widely held theory that dogs eat grass deliverately to induce vomiting.

Great Dane

GREAT DANE: "Giant" is a more applicable word than "great" for this dog, and how it came to be connected with Denmark is a mystery, since the breed apparently originated in Germany and was certainly brought to its peak of perfection there. It is of the Mastiff family, with a typically heavy head, and was used in times past to track and fight wild boars.

A mammoth dog (at least 28 inches high at the shoulders and preferably more and weighing from 120 to 150 pounds) there are some caveats, in addition to its size, to

be observed by the prospective owner. While eminently trainable, because it is alert and perceptive, the job is not easy for the amateur: because of the Great Dane's size it may inadvertently knock small children down when it is playing; its tail is sensitive and subject to injury; and the heart and kidney diseases to which it is prey may shorten its life. Withal, the Great Dane is a fine house and guard dog. For show purposes a wide variety of coat colors are permissible: blue, black, brindle, fawn, or harlequin. (Working: 1–2–3; Nonsporting:4)

GREAT PYRENEES: The Pyrenean Mountain Dog, as it is known in England and on the Continent, is an ancient breed whose fossil remains date back to the Bronze Age. At least as early as the fifteenth century, French and Spanish shepherds in the Pyrenees used this breed, equipped with a spiked iron collar, to protect their flocks against wolves and bears. In 1675 a Pyrenean caught the eye of Louis XIV, and the breed promptly became a favorite of French royalty. In more recent times these big dogs have proved

*Great Pyrenees or
Pyrenean Mountain Dog*

themselves not only as affectionate companions but as adept and eager pullers of carts and sleds.

Though massive (25 to 32 inches tall; and from 90 to 125 pounds), these white dogs with bearlike coats have smaller appetites than other breeds of comparable size. (Working: 1–2–3; Nonsporting: 4)

Greyhound

GREYHOUND: A tomb carving in the Nile Valley, circa 4,000 B.C., pictures a Greyhound. The breed has changed very little since ancient Egyptian times. What it hunted in those days we don't know, but in more modern times it has been used to overtake deer, foxes, and hares. The speediest of all dogs (it has been clocked at 37 m.p.h.), it is now used extensively for racing or coursing.

Medium-sized (60 to 70 pounds, and 25 to 30 inches tall), this dog with a smooth, short coat of any color is high-strung and not over affectionate and consequently it is not a good pet for small children. As a hunter, it is a sight hound without a particularly keen sense of smell. (Hound: 1–2–3–4)

GREYHOUND COURSING: a competition matching the speed and skill of one Greyhound against another. A brace of hounds are released to chase a hare (in the United States a jackrabbit is used) that has been given a head start in a fenced course or open area. In this test of speed, which is not really a hunt, most hares escape unharmed.

GREYHOUND RACING: a sport nearly one hundred years old in which Greyhounds, sprung from a starting gate much like those used for horse races, chase a mechanical rabbit for fun, fame, and sometimes fortune for their owners.

GRIFFON: see *Pointing Wirehaired Griffon.*

A field of Greyhounds breaks from the starting gate.

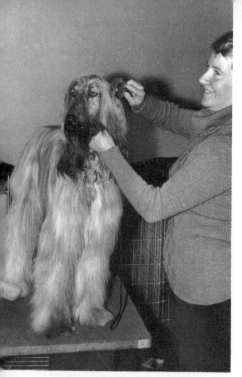

condition. In general, dogs with long coats need to be brushed or combed daily, while short-coated ones require grooming far less frequently. Many breeds develop snarls or mats that must be teased out or in some cases cut off with a scissors. Care should be taken to prevent cutting the skin.

Most dogs greatly enjoy being brushed or combed and have a great distaste for being bathed. Luckily for them, baths are needed only at infrequent intervals, particularly if they spend much of their lives outdoors. (See also *baths*.)

Since grooming differs from breed to breed and since an enormous variety of brushes, mitts, combs, and other utensils are available, a dog owner should acquire a book or a set of grooming instructions for his own breed, available in most book and pet shops. These manuals will also

GRIFFON BRUXELLOIS: see *Brussels Griffon*.

GRIZZLE: bluish-gray color.

GROOMING: All dogs require a degree of grooming, both for the sake of appearance and also to maintain coat and skin in a healthy

Three popular type brushes.

110

explain the far more intricate tonsorial and cosmetic procedures that must be followed if a dog is to enter a show ring.

GROUPS: classifications into which recognized breeds are divided by major kennel clubs throughout the world. In the United States and Canada all dogs are divided into six groups: Sporting, Hounds, Working Dogs, Terriers, Toys, and Nonsporting Dogs (though the lastnamed contains a few entrants who are distinctly "sporting"). For the most part, breeds recognized in the United States are recognized in Canada, and vice versa, but there are some exceptions. Breeds newly recognized by one of these countries are not automatically accepted across the border.

In England dogs are classified into two major groups—Sporting Breeds and Nonsporting Breeds. Each is subclassified as follows: under Sporting are listed Hounds, Gundogs, and Terriers; under Nonsporting come the Utility, Working, and Toy groups.

Australia classes the breeds as follows: Toys, Sporting Terriers, Gundogs, Hounds, Working Dogs, and Nonsporting Dogs.

Breed classifications in each of these areas are indicated beneath entries in this book.

Working Dog

St. Bernard

Terrier

Irish Terrier

Hound

Bassett Hound

Sporting or Gundog

Labrador Retreiver

Toy

Pekinese

Nonsporting or Utility

Bulldog

GUARD DOGS: dogs that perform their duties in private homes and apartments, on farms, for a variety of commercial enterprises such as factories, warehouses, and department stores, and at border crossing points between countries. Any family pet that instinctively becomes vocal when strangers approach its domain is a serviceable watchdog, no matter what its size. Most dogs who work as guards are of large breeds traditionally associated with sentry and guard work, though any dog with a sufficient span of attention can be trained for such purposes. Police forces often have dogs trained for attack as well as guard functions, as do nations at war. Professionally trained guard dogs are a poor risk as pets.

GUIDE DOGS: dogs trained for use by the blind in the United States, where a school for guide dogs was begun in 1926, and in Great Britain. Several such centers now exist in both countries. Dogs who are easily trainable, eager to please, even-tempered, and of sufficient size to make their directives quickly recognized by their blind owners go through an intensive period of training at a "school." Once graduated, they are brought together with their prospective blind masters for additional coordinated training.

Here an instructor is teaching Seeing Eye dogs and their potential owners the technique of crossing streets together.

GUMS: the hard tissue that covers the lower part of the teeth and protects the roots and bony socket from invasion by bacteria from the mouth. To keep the gums firm and healthy, dogs should be given hard biscuits to chew; all tartar should be removed regularly, especially in middle and old age. Diseased gums are a common cause of bad breath. The gums separate from the jawbone, and pockets of pus form that cause loosening of the teeth and may spread to infect the heart or kidneys or other organs of the body.

GUNDOG: any Pointer, Retriever, Setter or Spaniel.

British children who watched the TV program "Blue Peter" collected enough money to buy and train Honey, a guide dog for the blind, shown here proudly guarding her litter of nine pups.

Tessa, an English Springer Spaniel, marches her pups off to early Field Trial training while her owner, writer and gundog expert, Macdonald Hastings, supervises operations.

GUNDOGS, EARLY TRAINING: Puppies can be "yard broken" —taught to heel, sit and stay, and obey a whistle command—and made "field-wise"—taught to wriggle under fences, find shallow stream crossings, etc.—at a very early age as long as training sessions are very brief, repeated frequently, and made coincidental with the puppy's routine pleasures. Pups can also be exposed to the scent of the kind of game they will later be called upon to hunt. Seri-

ous, formal training should not begin until the puppy is eight months old.

GUNDOG WORKING TESTS: tests conducted in England, chiefly to keep gundogs from forgetting their lessons during the off-season for shooting live birds and game. Dummies or cold game are used under artificial conditions on a preset course that is identical for every dog competing. Such tests are held only for Retrievers and Spaniels.

H

HACKLES: the hair on a dog's neck and back, which rises involuntarily when the dog is angry or frightened.

HACKNEY ACTION: raising of the front feet high, considered wasted motion in a dog and a faulty gait.

Hairless Dog

HAIRLESS DOGS: There are many varieties scattered around the world. The best-known breed, the Mexican Hairless, was once fairly popular but is now granted recognition only in Canada. Hairlessness perhaps results from a blood deficiency, and in many cases all but the dog's front teeth may be missing. Hairless dogs are known by such exotic names as the African Sand Dog, the Turkish Naked Dog, the Chinese Crested Dog, and, in Mexico, the hairless Xoloitzcuintli.

HANDLERS: Professionals who are licensed to exhibit at shows dogs belonging to others, or to board, groom, train, and transport dogs to shows where they exhibit them for their owners.

HARDMOUTHED: given to biting down on or mutilating the game retrieved.

HARD PAD DISEASE: a virus infection causing hardening of the skin of the foot pads and nose. At one time this was considered a separate disease, but it is now recognized as an epidemic symptom of canine distemper.

HAREFOOT: an elongated oval foot.

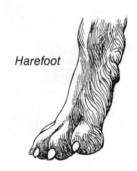

Harefoot

HARELIP: see *cleft palate.*

HARLEQUIN: having patched or piebald coloring, most often black on white.

HARNESS: a double leather collar with one band low around the neck, the other around the chest, fastened at the top with a ring over the withers.

Dog Harness

HARRIER: Perhaps the only breed specifically developed to hunt hares, the first recorded pack dates back to 1260. These Hounds were originally large and badger or pure white in color and rather slow of foot. Crosses with other Hound breeds gave them their present black, tan, and white tricolor, which is characteristic,

Harrier

though some have a unique blue-mottled shade. They are midway between the English Foxhound and the Beagle in size—19 to 21 inches tall. (Hound: 1–2–3–4)

HAUNCH: buttock or rump.

HAW: a membrane in the inside corner of the eye, red in color.

HEARING: Dogs hear high-pitched sounds better than humans, at a greater distance, and have superior ability to place the location from which a sound comes. Keenness of hearing varies considerably from breed to breed, as well as individually. Dogs with large, erect, uncropped ears have an advantage. Puppies are deaf at birth and do not begin to develop sensitivity to sounds until they are from ten to twelve days old.

HEART DISEASE: should be suspected whenever a dog tires easily after normal exercise or develops an upper respiratory cough when active or quiet. Restlessness at night is another suggested symptom. Heart disease may be congenital, or caused by heartworms, old age, or complications from other diseases. Many congenital heart ailments can now be corrected by surgery. A veterinarian can refer you to a specialist. Most heart diseases can be controlled by properly supervised medication and special diets, thereby enabling an afflicted dog to enjoy a long and comfortable life. Sudden violent activity is as bad for old dogs as for old people.

HEARTWORMS: worms transmitted to dogs by mosquitoes that have bitten an already infected dog. Adult worms come to rest in the heart where they inhibit circulation. An affected dog may cough, lose weight no matter how much you feed it, and collapse after rigorous exercise. A dog that hunts or works in a mosquito-infested area is a logical target. Symptoms of the affliction are easily confused with those of other ailments. A veterinarian can make a blood test that will identify the problem, and will most likely be able to suggest a remedy and prevention of further problems.

HEAT, or OESTRUS (also referred to as "In" or "On Season"): the period during which ovulation occurs in the bitch, making her receptive to male dogs. In most bitches it occurs twice a year but in some breeds may vary from four to twelve months. The duration is approximately three weeks.

First signs: The bitch becomes restless. The vulva begins to swell. Shortly afterward, a heavy blood discharge appears (first day of heat), which continues for about ten days and is followed by a scantier, light-colored discharge lasting eight to ten days. Bitches usually conceive between the ninth and fourteenth days of heat, but considerable variations have been observed.

A bitch in season that is not mated must be carefully watched. She attracts male dogs and may find exits from a home or kennel that the owner never knew existed. Her odor can be reduced (but *not* eliminated) by a suitable dose of chlorophyll and by sprinkling a strong disinfectant on the spot where the dog has urinated.

Small pet bitches should be kept indoors where they can use newspapers for urinating and defecating. Comfortable belts with a pocket for disposable tissues are available and prevent staining of rugs and upholstery. In urban areas, a boarding kennel may be the answer. If a bitch is never to be bred, spaying is recommended. Contrary to popular myth, the operation does not make bitches fat or lethargic; overfeeding is generally to blame.

HEATING: Dogs need less warmth than humans, and thick-coated ones naturally get along far better in cold weather than do Toys or short-coated animals. Many breeders of Retrievers, for example, keep their dogs out in cold weather to ensure that their animals have a good coat. In sub-freezing temperatures, however, all but Malamutes and the like need to come indoors at night or to sleep in heated kennels. Bitches with a litter of new puppies, as well as elderly dogs or those suffering from illnesses particularly need warm surroundings.

HEMATOMA OF THE EAR: a condition in which a major blood vessel in the earflap is ruptured. It appears as a large soft swelling. Hematoma is a complication of many ear diseases and is caused by shaking or rubbing the head against a hard object.

HEMORRHAGE: severe bleeding either from a visible external injury or from internal bleeding into a body cavity. In either case, quick action is essential.

External bleeding: A severed artery spurts jets of bright red blood; a vein emits a steady flow of darker blood. What to do:

1. Since the dog will be frightened or in pain, or both, tie the dog's mouth shut to prevent panic biting. Use any material that comes to hand, wrapping it several times around the muzzle, but making sure the dog can breathe. If possible, get help to enable you to keep the dog lying prone.

2. Attempt to slow the flow of blood by applying a tourniquet or by pressing the pressure points to close off a blood vessel temporarily. Somewhere between the dog's heart and the site of the injury there will be a spot where applied pressure will slow bleeding. Search for the pressure point until you find it.

3. Get the dog to a veterinary hospital as quickly as possible. If the injury takes place away from home, you will almost certainly need assistance: police or even total strangers may be willing to lend a hand.

Internal bleeding: This can be just as severe and as quickly fatal. It is much harder for a nonprofessional to diagnose, however. Feebleness, cold ears and feet, rapid and shallow breathing, and shivering are some of the symptoms. Cover the dog with anything handy to keep it warm, lift it as gently as possible onto any carrier, the firmer the better, though an old blanket that can be used as a hammock will do, and get it to a veterinarian with all possible speed.

HEPATITIS: inflammation of the liver. It may be caused by a virus (infectious hepatitis or Rubarth's disease), bacteria, parasites, or poisons. It is always serious and must be treated by a veterinarian.

HEREDITARY DEFECTS: physical defects transmitted from one generation to the next through genes. Not every puppy in a litter shows signs of the defect, but many of them will be carriers and pass the abnormality on to their progeny. Common hereditary conditions include:

1. Progressive retinal atrophy (see *eye diseases*).

2. Entropion and ectropion (see *eye diseases*).

3. Cleft palate and harelip (in short-nosed dogs such as Boston Terriers and Pekingese).

4. Elbow dysplasia.

5. Hip dysplasia: a malformation of the joint between the ball-like head of the femur (thighbone) and its socket in the pelvis. It has been recognized in almost all the larger breeds except the racing Greyhound. Hip dysplasia usually does not show up when a dog is young, but as the disease progresses it can lead to pain, lameness, or crippling arthritis. However, the early stage of joint deterioration can be diagnosed by x-rays at two years of age.

Responsible breeders are attempting to eliminate dysplasia from their kennels and have all their breeding stock x-rayed by a veterinarian. In the United Kingdom and the United States the x-rays can be sent to a panel of experts for official certification. There is no cure for hip dysplasia, but techniques recently developed allow a pet dog to lead a relatively pain-free life.

HERNIA (rupture): a break in the muscles of the abdominal wall that allows the internal organs to drop

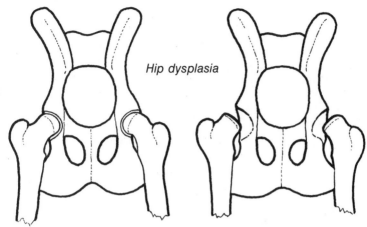

Hip dysplasia

Correct bone formation   *Typical malformation*

through and lie under the skin, forming a pocket. There are four common types of hernias in dogs and most can be repaired by surgery.

1. *Umbilical* hernia (open belly-button) is present at birth, usually contains fat, and may close before the puppy is six months old.

2. *Inguinal* hernia is a gap between the belly and the hind leg.

3. *Perineal* hernia is found at the back part of the abdominal cavity. It appears as a large swelling on one or both sides of the anus, usually in dogs over eight years old. It may be caused by straining, enlarged prostate or· other disease.

4. *Diaphragmatic* hernia is a tear in the diaphragm (the large muscle separating the abdomen from the chest). It is almost always the result of an automobile accident.

HIP DYSPLASIA: see *hereditary defects*.

HOCK: several bones of the hind leg that form the joint between the metatarsus and the second thigh; the true heel.

HODGKIN'S DISEASE: a term loosely used to describe several forms of cancer of the lymph glands and bone marrow, such as lymphomatosis, lymphatic leukemia, and lymphosarcoma.

HOLLAND: the official canine authority is Raad van Beheer op Kynologisch Gebied, Emmalaan 16, NL, Amsterdam 2.

HONG KONG: write the Hong Kong Kennel Club, 9 Icehouse Street, Hong Kong, for information about canine matters in this distant corner of the globe.

HOOKWORMS *(ancylostoma canina* or *uncinaria):* microscopic worms. The adults live in the dog's small intestine where they lay hundreds of eggs. The eggs are passed in the feces and develop on the ground into larvae. When eaten by a dog, the larvae gradually return to the intestine. Puppies can become infected in the uterus before birth or by nursing.

Hookworms are bloodsuckers. In adult dogs they cause diarrhea and anemia, in puppies, indigestion, severe anemia, and even death. To prevent prenatal infection in puppies, it is essential to have a veterinarian check a bitch before she is bred, and treat her for hookworms if ova are found in the stool. It is probable that a hookworm vaccine will soon be perfected.

HOT CLIMATES: Dogs born in the tropics, or those taken from temperate zones to tropical areas, have a remarkable ability to adapt to the climate. Breeds with medium-length coats do better than those with short or long hair. All need more calories than in temperate areas. Insect pests (fleas, lice, and ticks) are far more numerous and heartworms (see entry) are prevalent. Dogs need to be kept in a screened area at the end of the day when mosquitoes are out.

HOT SPOTS (acute pyoderma): areas of moist eczema of the skin. They occur suddenly (often overnight) and develop rapidly into painful, weeping sores. Mild cases can be treated at home by clipping the hair and applying calamine lotion, but most dogs require the care of a veterinarian. The causes of the spots are varied and often cannot be determined. Hot spots are found in all breeds.

HOUND SHOWS: are held in various parts of the United States and the British Isles for Foxhounds, Bassets, Beagles, and Harriers, and are most often given under the auspices of clubs and associations that specialize in one or more breeds and keep their own registrations and studbooks. There are classes for one Hound, a couple, two couples, four couples, and eight couples, depending on the show. For the most part, such shows are for dogs who are field-proven.

HOUND TRAILS: A British sporting event for Foxhound-type dogs 18 to 24 inches tall and somewhat lighter in weight than customary for the breed. As many as ninety dogs may be let loose at the starting line to follow the scent of a "drag" laid down over a course about ten miles long for grown dogs, and five miles for puppies. The first dog over the finish line is the winner, with no handicaps asked or given.

HOUSEBREAKING: If you live in a house with easy access to the outdoors, you will want to train your puppy from the start to use the outside as its toilet. The rules are simple, the results not quite so predictable.

1. Take the pup outside within an hour after every meal, or at any other time you see it circling and sniffing, and early in the morning and just before you go to bed. When the dog cooperates, praise it warmly. On subsequent trips outdoors, always take it back to the same spot, which the pup will recognize as its own: but also let it nose around a little in case it wants to choose another. Take the pup inside at once after it has evacuated, so that it will connect going out with business, not pleasure.

2. Once indoors, keep the dog confined to a small area—a large

box or crate, or on a short rope or lead in the kitchen or other easily cleaned floor where you can keep an eye on it. Dogs instinctively refuse to foul their own nests, and the confined area you contrive is the nest. Take the pup out when it gets restless or cries, as well as at the times already indicated. *Don't* give the pup the run of the house.

3. If the pup makes a mistake, scold it gently if you catch it in the act, and scold it *immediately*. A three-minute wait is too long, since the dog won't understand why it is being scolded. Don't hit the dog or rub its nose in the mistake. It won't understand. Clean up immediately and use a disinfectant on the spot to obliterate the odor. Otherwise, the pup will return to it. Puppies have very little control of their bladder and bowels. They will make mistakes—less frequently as they get to be three or four months old and as you establish a routine by taking them out at specific hours of the day. You need to be kind but firm, infinitely patient, and alert to your pup's needs. As a grownup, depending on breed and individual differences, it will not need to go out more than two or three times a day.

If you live in an apartment, you may not always be able to get down to the street before nature has taken its course. Paper training is the answer. Some dogs of small breeds use newspapers all their lives as a toilet. With larger breeds paper training is an intermediate step to outdoors. As with outdoor training, patience and one's physical presence on the scene make the job easier.

Training goes much faster when a puppy is caught in the act.

1. Choose a small room in the apartment that can be closed off from all other areas and that has a linoleum, vinyl, or tile floor. Cover all but a small corner of it with several layers of newspapers. Put the pup's bed or box in the uncovered area. It will use the paper when it needs to urinate or defecate. Tell the pup it is a good dog whenever it uses the papers. Scold it gently if it makes a mistake and fails to use the newspaper. Gradually decrease the area on which you put down paper. Pick up the pup and set it on the remaining paper when it shows signs of wanting to urinate or defecate. Scold the pup verbally if it uses the floor, and clean up at once. With proper attention, it will soon be using only a small corner of the room as a toilet.

2. Don't make *any* exceptions to this program until your pup begins to get the idea. If you leave doors open and allow it to wander into the living room when nobody is there to watch it, you have only yourself to blame for mistakes and housebreaking will take a lot longer.

3. When and if you move from inside to outside, you'll have to start all over again. Your dog won't connect gutters with newspapers. At first, take with you on the walk a piece of newspaper and lay it down in the street close to the curb while you keep an eye on traffic. Set your pup on it and hope for the best. It may be nervous about strange noises, so be patient. Once the pup cooperates, tell it what a fine dog it is, gather up the paper, and deposit it in the nearest litter can or take it upstairs to your garbage container. Congratulate yourself and take a smaller piece of paper next time out. Before long you most probably can dispense with it completely.

Whether you are trying to housebreak your dog for indoor or outdoor purposes, don't leave it alone in the confined area for long periods. Go in and out of the room frequently, play with the pup, and talk to it to keep it feeling part of the family.

HUMANE SOCIETIES: These exist in the United States, England, and elsewhere to perform a variety of services allied to the well-being of animals, both domestic and those confined in zoos. In general, they operate independently of each other to prevent cruelty to animals, provide adoption services, and operate shelters for lost, unwanted, or stray, unlicensed, roaming dogs. Some societies have medical facilities, run obedience-training courses, are active in antivivisection movements, and maintain transient shelters at airports to care for animals arriving or departing by air.

HUNGARIAN PULI: see *Puli*.

HURDLE RACING: see *scent hurdle racing*.

HUSKY: see *Siberian Husky*.

HYDROPHOBIA: see *rabies*.

HYSTERIA: any uncontrolled excitement. It may be due to fright, thunderstorms, or many other causes. Owners can often stop a fit of hysterical barking by tapping the dog's nose smartly with a rolled-up newspaper and then calming it down with gentle handling.

I

IBIZAN HOUND: A scenthound that looks like a cross between a Borzoi and a Foxhound, it is apparently a native of Spain and takes its name from the Balearic island of Ibiza. The dog points and retrieves a variety of game, either singly or in a pack. These animals (23 to 26 inches at the withers) are remarkable high jumpers and bright and better house dogs than most pack hounds. Their coats can be smooth, wiry, or long; solid red, tawny, or white, or a mix of white and one of these two colors. (Hound: 2)

Ibizan Hound

ICELAND DOG: A member of the Spitz family, the breed seems to have been brought to Iceland by early Norwegian settlers. These canines worked for centuries as farm dogs—as useful for keeping domestic animals *out* of areas where they weren't wanted as for herding them into areas where they were. This medium-sized dog (15 to 18 inches tall and weighing some 30 pounds) has been bred in England since World War I days. It has a hard, medium-long coat that is white with fawn markings or light fawn or golden. (Utility: 2)

IMMUNITY: A dog is said to be immune to a disease when its blood contains sufficient anti-bodies to prevent infection. Immunity follows recovery from certain diseases or may be induced with vaccines. Immunity may also be transferred into mother's milk, which will protect the puppy for several weeks after its birth.

INBREEDING: the mating of close relatives—mother and son or brother and sister. Most experts take a negative view of this, except in controlled scientific experiments, since if both parents carry a defective gene, even a recessive one, it will show up as a defect in about 25 percent of the litter. Non-professionals are advised not to breed dogs in this fashion, or to buy an inbred puppy.

INDIA: The Kennel Club of India adheres closely to United Kingdom standards and is located at Vilayet Manzil, Begampet, Deccan, Andhra Pradesh.

INFERTILITY: the inability of a dog or bitch to produce puppies after mating. It should not be confused with the inability to mate. In the male dog sterility may be due to bruising or infection of the testicles, hormone imbalance, or many other conditions. Common causes in the bitch include cysts and other diseases of the ovary or infection of the uterus. Some cases of infertility can be cured, but many are due to irreversible changes in the reproductive organs.

INFRARED LIGHTS: useful over a whelping box if your house is poorly heated and you need to keep puppies warm. Make sure it is hung high enough above the box so that the cord is out of easy chewing range.

INSURANCE: If you have a homeowner's policy, it probably protects you against a dog's potential misbehavior—digging up the neighbor's flower bed or biting his son—but as with all insurance policies, one needs to read the fine print. Accident and life insurance policies (except for death from disease or natural causes) are available, but the costs are very high. Check an insurance broker for details. In shipping a dog by air, land, or sea, insurance for the trip can usually be purchased at reasonable rates.

INTERBREEDING: the mating of dogs of different breeds, usually to introduce a particularly desirable trait or traits.

INTERDIGITAL CYSTS: small, pimplelike sores between the toes. They frequently rupture and cause pain and lameness. The exact cause cannot always be determined, but may be due to bacteria, mites, or fungi. Long-term treatment is often necessary and should be started as early as possible, before the sores become chronic.

IRELAND: The Irish Kennel Club has its headquarters at 4 Harcourt St., Dublin, 2.

Irish Setter

IRISH SETTER: "Big Red," who was more white than red when it first appeared in Ireland nearly two centuries ago, has risen rapidly in popularity in recent years and is now among the top five in number of registrations in the United States. It is among the most beautiful of gundogs and almost appears to realize it: artists around the world have painted the dog as it freezes—head up, one paw lifted, tail straight out, and the entire body rigid in a classic hunting pose. Like certain nonanimal celebrities, the Irish Setter may at times prove temperamental, loaded with charm, and something of a clown. It moves with dazzling

A Setter in action

speed, and when the dog decides to wander, it is very likely to find itself many miles from hearth and home in short order. The big dog needs a firm and patient trainer, and once its native stubbornness is overcome, Big Red becomes a fine pet and a spectacular performer in the show ring. Adult dogs are from 24 to 26 inches in height and weigh from 55 to 60 pounds; bitches are a bit less. The coat should be straight, predominantly deep chestnut and not black. (Sporting: 1–3; Gundog: 2–4)

IRISH TERRIER: This dog is a typical Irishman—intrepid and obdurate, warm-hearted and contentious, whimsical and often unpredictable. Once one of these handsome little animals makes up its mind on a course of action, a strong-minded trainer is needed to convince it to change it. They are fine hunters and swimmers, fearless and inquisitive, devoted to their owners, and as often as not a bit bellicose when other dogs are on the scene. A true terrier in every sense of the word, the "daredevil" is a cocky and alert animal whose dense wiry coat is red-gold, but can range from a bright red to a

Irish Terrier

This 1820 etching calls the dog an Irish Greyhound. Obviously, it is far closer to today's Irish Wolfhound.

wheaten shade. Dogs stand around 18 inches at the withers and range in weight from 25 to 27 pounds. (Terrier: 1–2–3–4)

Irish Water Spaniel

IRISH WATER SPANIEL: Unique on at least two counts—as the possessor of a rattail and a topknot that peaks between the eyes—this breed, which has been known in Ireland for more than two hundred years, has a host of appealing attributes. The dogs are cheerful clowns, unexcelled swimmers, great retrievers of ducks in water, and have good noses and lively intelligence. Their dark liver coats are curly, with tight ringlets on much of the body, and are naturally oily to repel water. Tallest of the Spaniels, they run from 21 to 24 inches in height and weigh between 45 and 65 pounds. (Sporting: 1–3; Gundogs: 2–4)

IRISH WOLFHOUND: Beneath its shaggy brow and limpid eye lurks the mind and soul of a lapdog, for this biggest of all breeds has over the centuries developed an unquenchable passion for children and adults alike. Irish lore and the records of ancient Greece and Rome tell of the exploits of the Wolfhounds who hunted wolves, Irish elk, and other big game, but

126

Irish Wolfhound

ancient Roman warning, *"Cave canem!"* (Beware the dog) was a polite reminder, not that the dog was ferocious, but that the owners had a pint-sized Italian Greyhound they didn't want a bumbling, heavy-footed guest to step on.

in our time these amiable giants essentially serve as gentle and affectionate companions and instant attention-getters in the show ring. People *do* keep them in apartments and small houses, but this is a bit risky since one wave of the tail is likely to sweep an entire tabletop clean. Dogs in the United States must be at least 32 inches in height at the shoulder and weigh not less than 120 pounds; in Great Britain a somewhat smaller and lighter dog is recognized. In both areas bitches are a bit smaller, not less than 105 pounds in America, 90 in England. (Hound: 1–2–3–4)

ISRAEL: The Canaan dog is only one of Israel's native breeds. For information write the Israel Kennel Club, P.O. Box 33055, Tel Aviv.

ITALIAN GREYHOUND: Known for more than two thousand years in much the same conformation, this dog is a mini-version of the Greyhound and has always been more pet than sportsman. Its ideal weight is under 10 pounds, and one authority believes that the

When an Irish Wolfhound decides to get friendly, it often forgets it is nearly seven-feet tall.

Italian Greyhound

These dogs (13 to 15 inches tall) have short, satiny coats of almost any color, although black and tan Terrier markings are frowned on for show purposes. Puppies must be carefully tended to keep them from becoming nervous and temperamental as adults; thus, they are not ideal as pets for small children. (Toy: 1–2–3–4)

ITALIAN SPINONE: The result of crosses between long-established Italian native hound breeds produced today's big dog with a rough coat, docked tail, and long ears, which is an all-purpose but somewhat slow gundog. Height is from 23 to 27½ inches, weight from 62 to 80 pounds. The dog should be pure white or white with brown or orange markings. (M: 1; Gundog: 2)

ITALY: the Italian Kennel Club is known as the Ente Nazionale della Cinofilia Italiana. Address: Viale Premuda 21,1-20129, Milano.

Italian Spinone

J

JACK RUSSELL TERRIER: No kennel club recognizes this dog as a breed, but in Great Britain the gay and spirited little terrier has long enjoyed considerable popularity. The name derives from a Devon parson who had a pack of hounds he used for foxes. He liked wirehaired breeds with medium-long legs, and whenever he found a good specimen, he added it to his pack. The present crossbreed has smoother hair, goes to ground or catches rats (as did his forebears), is friendly and alert. Jack Russells are about 13 inches at the withers and weigh about 15 pounds.

Jack Russell Terrier

JAPAN: The Japan Dog Federation, 9-8, 3-chome, Uchi-Kanda, Chiyodaku, Tokyo, is the official arbiter on canine matters in the land of the Rising Sun.

JAPANESE FIGHTING DOG: Called the Tosa, this Mastiff-like animal is now used for guard duties and over the years has been transformed into a devoted, if somewhat formidable looking, house pet.

Japanese Spaniel

JAPANESE SPANIEL: This tiny dog, also known as the Japanese Chin, is most probably related to the Pug and the Pekingese. Its ancestry dates back many centuries, but it didn't make an appearance in the Western world until after the middle of the nineteenth century. While the dog's average weight is around 7 pounds, many prized Japanese Spaniels have weighed considerably less. The lush-coated little dogs are snub-nosed, and the nose color should

Judging of Toy dogs usually is done on a table or raised platform.

match the coat—black in a black and white dog, rose-colored in a red and white animal. All in all, the Chin is a most stylish and tough-minded Oriental. (Toy: 1–2–3–4)

JAUNDICE: a yellow coloration of the whites of the eye, mouth, and, later, of the entire body. The yellowing is due to the presence of bile pigment in the blood stream. Jaundice is always a serious condition. It can follow improper use of worm medicines, certain liver diseases, or the excessive destruction of the red cells in the blood.

JUDGE: in the show ring, the individual licensed by the governing kennel club to judge dogs and make awards under various classifications. At shows, each dog is examined and evaluated against the standards for its own breed as well as the merits or demerits of other competitors. Such examina-

tions include inspection of the dog's head, body, general conformation and gait, muscular development, teeth, and a score or more elements.

While judging procedures vary somewhat around the world, the underlying basis for granting awards is much the same in every country. If a judge feels that none of the animals he is judging measure up to the perfect standard, he may withhold all or some of the awards.

In most shows in the United States and elsewhere breed winners go on to compete against other winners in their group—one Toy winner against all others, etc., with the winners in each group competing for the ultimate honor, best in show.

In field trials the judges grant awards to the dog or dogs that perform most successfully the assignments given them.

130

JUNIOR SHOWMANSHIP: This is a special feature of dog shows in the United States, Canada, and Mexico, which gives youngsters a chance to measure their ring-skills as handlers against others in their age group. There are two divisions, one for boys and girls ten to twelve years old, a second for those thirteen to sixteen years old. There are also novice and open divisions, and the first place open winners become eligible to compete for a national championship in the United States. These contests test the ability of young people as handlers, not the merits of the dogs they are showing.

A junior handler displays the fine points of her Basset Hound at an all-breed show in Wisconsin. Cheryl's Hound was either bored or sleepy—probably both.

K

KARELIAN BEAR DOG: Another variety of the Spitz family, it is used to hunt bear and elk in the Karelian district of northeast Europe. As a pet, it is less than ideal—stubborn and with an inherent dislike for all other dogs.

Keeshond

KEESHOND: Known as Keeshonden in the United States, the name came from Kees (pronounced "Kays") de Gyselaer, who led the Dutch Patriot party in a struggle against the Prince of Orange in the years following the French Revolution. "Kees' hound" became the symbol of that party and rescued the breed from a life it had led for centuries—as watchdogs living on barges that plied the canals of Holland.

Strictly a pet, this 18-inch dog with a dense grayish coat wears a distinctive pair of spectacles—unique markings around its eyes that make it unmistakable. Its ruff is almost as impressive as a lion's mane, and the plumed tail, which lies over the back, imparts a distinct note of elegance. (Nonsporting: 1–3; Utility: 2)

KENNEL CLUB: one of the regulatory bodies existing in many countries to register dogs, supervise field and show events, license judges and handlers, approve standards for old breeds and new as they are recognized, and provide help and information to dog owners.

KENNEL CLUB, ENGLISH: For just over a century *the* Kennel Club has ruled British dogdom without opposition or competition. Its registration roster contains the names of over two million pedigreed dogs and the Club each year registers close to 200,000 additional names.

The Kennel Club stages Cruft's Show itself and casts a benevolent eye on nearly 4,000 other shows, matches, and trials that are held each twelve months under the auspices of upwards of 1,600 registered societies, each of which recognizes the Club as its jurisdictional overseer. A long list of committees and sub-committees, comprised of voluntary workers for the most part, helps the Kennel Club supervise canine matters that range from the exportation of British breeds to the apprehension of persons guilty of cruelty or neglect to dogs. Dishonesty, faking, prejudice in judging, and "discreditable conduct" of any nature are also matters presided over by the Club, which has the power to fine, discipline, or disbar in perpetuity the guilty parties.

Dog show entries in Great Britain as well as registration fees are miniscule, ten to thirty percent of those charged in the United States.

Address: 1–4 Clarges St., London WI.

KENNEL COUGH (infectious tracheobronchitis): a highly infectious disease of dogs of all ages. Except when they are coughing, dogs are alert and well. With proper treatment recovery is usual, but may take up to four weeks. No effective vaccine is currently available. Control of its spreading to other dogs in the kennel depends to some extent on adequate sanitation.

KENNEL NAME: the formal name under which dogs are registered in the country of their birth. The first name, or prefix, may come with the puppy's papers if it is bought from a breeder who has registered that prefix. Suppose you buy your dog from a hypothetical Vermilion Kennel. When you register the puppy, he will be Vermilion's Jester or whatever second name you want. For registration purposes, a dog's name cannot duplicate one already registered. In most countries the length of a dog's name is limited to a stipulated number of letters, usually 20 to 30.

KERATITIS (blue-eye): inflammation of the cornea—the transparent membrane covering the iris and pupil—in which the cornea becomes discolored. The white of the eye may or may not become reddish. This condition is serious and requires diagnosis and treatment.

Kerry Blue Terrier

KERRY BLUE TERRIER: A longtime favorite in Ireland, where the breed has been known for more than a hundred years, this dog is a hunter of small game, a land and water retriever, a herder, and, in recent years, primarily a good companion. In England and the United States the Kerry's coat must be carefully trimmed for show; in Ireland, no tampering with his soft, wavy blue coat is allowed. Puppies of this medium-sized breed (17½ to 19½ inches tall; 29 to 40 pounds) are born black and become lighter as they mature. Some say the dog has a temper that blazes up now and then. Perhaps this lack of inhibition is what makes him one of the most

133

long-lived of all known breeds. (Terrier: 1–2–3–4)

KIDNEY DISEASES: common in dogs, especially males over five years of age. The first sign is often an increase in thirst. A veterinarian can diagnose kidney disease by laboratory tests of urine and blood, and advise the proper medication and special diets.

KING CHARLES SPANIEL: see *English Toy Spaniel.*

KNUCKLING OVER: having a weak, double-jointed wrist that causes the joint to double forward when the dog is standing. Swelling of the bones at the joint is sometimes apparent.

Komondor

KOMONDOR: Used as a guard dog for sheep and cattle in Hungary for centuries, this large, shaggy white dog with its unique matted or corded coat that virtually disguises it from head to tail tip, is a tough, courageous guardian. It is, by preference, a hard worker who spends most of the time outdoors where the heavy coat protects it not only against the weather but from attackers. A big dog (a minimum of 23½ inches tall for bitches, with males weighing up to 90 pounds), it has no sense of humor if it feels the herd or its human family is being attacked. (Working: 1–2)

Kuvasz

KUVASZ: Known in Great Britain as the Hungarian Kuvasz, this dog's ancestors were huge beasts who apparently came from Tibet. Hungarian nobles bred the dogs for boar hunting and guardian duties on their estates as early as the fifteenth century, and these white animals with long, somewhat wavy coats have been unexcelled farm and guard dogs ever since. Present specimens range in height from 24 to 26 inches at the shoulder and weight from 60 to 70 pounds. A methodical dog, the Kuvasz appears to size up people as either friends or enemies on first acquaintance. Once it has decided what category they belong in, it neither forgets nor changes its mind. The dog thus requires careful upbringing as a pup and affectionate handling as an adult if it is to be a good family companion. (Working: 1–2–3).

L

LABRADOR RETRIEVER: Most popular of all Retrievers, the Labrador combines keen scent and a fondness for water with a prodigious ability to find and retrieve upland game. The muscular and compact animal descended from large Newfoundland dogs, and for nearly two centuries has excelled as a worker and house pet. It has starred in the show ring, and its great endurance and trainability cause it to be eagerly sought after as a guide dog for the blind and for police and guard work. Dogs are 21½ to 24½ inches at the shoulder, bitches about an inch less; and the Lab's weight can range from 55 to 75 pounds. The short, hard coat can be black, chocolate, or yellow, often with a small white spot on the chest. (Sporting: 1–3; Gundog: 2–4)

Labrador Retriever

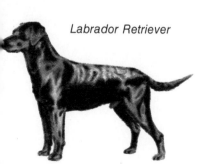

LADIES KENNEL ASSOCIATION: An early feminist effort, this British association was founded late in the nineteenth century at a time when activities in the world of dogs were dominated by men. Over the years it pretty well eliminated male chauvinism in dogdom. Today the early winter L.K.A. show in London continues to be one of the most popular of all canine events in the United Kingdom.

Lakeland Terrier

LAKELAND TERRIER: Originally a working Terrier, which meant that it was a fearless hunter of foxes and badgers in England, the bewhiskered and debonair Lakeland has lost some of its popularity in recent years. This is hard to explain, for the dog has vast charm, is a loyal and dependable guardian, and can be gay and entertaining without becoming as vocal as some of the other Terrier breeds. It is only 13 to 15 inches in height, weighs about 17 pounds, and has a double coat—hard and wiry on the outside, soft underneath. Colors range from black to wheaten. (Terrier: 1–2–3–4)

LEASH, or **LEAD:** Puppies should become accustomed to a collar and leash (or lead, as it is also called) at from two to three months of age, not for true training purposes, but so they can get used to the sensation. The pup will most likely submit to the indignity of a collar at first and then balk after it is dragged along for a few steps. At this point it should be released, and the same procedure followed the next day. Often, early lead training will proceed much more smoothly if one follows after the puppy until it has become familiar with the feeling of the collar and lead. Real training should begin when the puppy is four to six months of age. (See also *obedience training*.)

LEATHER: the earflap.

LEONBERGER: One of the lesser-known breeds, and officially recognized only in England, the name stems from *Leo* (the lion). For decades St. Bernards, Newfoundlands, and Pyrenean Mountain Dogs were crossed and recrossed in an effort to produce a dog that resembled the king of the forest. Today the Leonberger looks like a dog, and a very handsome one to boot, who bears a distinct resemblance to a Golden

Leonberger

Retriever. It is a big dog, 27 to 30 inches at the shoulder, and is adaptable and affectionate, save for some initial suspicion toward strangers. (Utility: 2)

LEPTOSPIROSIS: A worldwide disease caused by several species of spirochetes. It may be mild or severe. One form (canicola) attacks the kidneys. Another (icterohemorragica) attacks the liver and intestines.

Prevention: Multivalent bacterins are available and are usually included in a puppy's immunization program. To ensure maximum protection, Hunting dogs should be vaccinated every year, three to four weeks before the beginning of the hunting season.

Spread: Via the urine of infected or recovered dogs; also through ponds contaminated with rat urine. Transmission to man has been recorded, but is rare. However, great care must be exercised in treating this disease at home.

Diagnosis: Can be confirmed with a blood test.

LEVEL BACK: a straight line from withers to base of the tail.

LEVEL BITE: front teeth of upper and lower jaws meeting edge to edge.

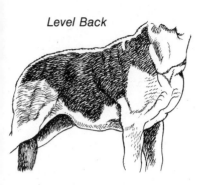

Level Back

LHASA APSO: A native of Tibet, where extremes of temperature are common and threats to the household often more so, this little dog was used inside the house to warn of intruders. The outside guards were traditionally ferocious Tibetan Mastiffs. Today the Lhasa Apso's intelligence and beauty have caused it to grow rapidly in popularity as a house pet. The diminutive dogs range from 10 to 11 inches at the withers (bitches slightly less) and the coat, which reaches the ground, is generally golden, but sometimes parti-colored. Considerable brushing is required. (Nonsporting: 1–4; Utility: 2; Terrier: 3)

Lhasa Apso

LICE: insect pests that spend their entire life on a dog's body, laying their eggs in the animal's hair. They can move from one dog to another, but not to humans. The ugly little parasites can be eliminated (but not easily) by insecti-cide powders, but are more often eliminated by medication.

LIFE SPAN: Generalizing, it may be said that small dogs can live to the age of twenty, middling-sized dogs to fifteen, and the large breeds only ten to twelve. The smallest of the Toy breeds, however, are short-lived while many big dogs have delighted their owners by living to what was for their breed an incredible span of years. More positively it can be stated that medical progress, combined with better nutritional standards and improved sanitation, have lengthened the life span of dogs remarkably, just as they have with human beings.

The old cliché that one year in a dog's life equals seven of a human life has no basis in fact.

Louse

LINEBREEDING: the mating of two dogs of the same breed that are related—but more distantly than father and daughter or mother and son. The object of this is to produce outstanding specimens of the breed by preserving the best qualities of an illustrious ancestor while eliminating less favorable ones.

LION DOG: See *Lowchen*.

LITTER: the puppies produced by a bitch at a single birth. Record litters range up to nineteen puppies for big dogs as against eleven

Six pups represent just about the average size litter for Pointers and other medium breeds.

for Toys. The average litter is around half that number, and birth of a single pup is by no means uncommon.

LOST DOGS: While dogs have excellent homing instincts, they sometimes wander too far away to find their way back. Make sure your dog wears a collar with tags on it giving your name and address, your dog's license number, and proof of rabies immunization. In many areas you can have a dog tattooed on the flank with a number that is nationally registered. The process is painless, and in case the animal is dognapped, one stands a good chance of getting it back. Animal shelters search for such tattoos, reputable pet stores will not resell such dogs, and research centers will not purchase them for experimentation.

The Canadian Kennel Club registers nose prints of dogs—an identification almost as positive as fingerprints for humans. Putting advertisements in local newspapers, announcements on local radio stations, and alerting local police headquarters and humane societies and shelters are other measures that can be taken.

Lowchen

LOWCHEN: The little "Lion Dog" is recognized in Great Britain. Shaved so as to have only a mane and tail tuft, it does indeed resemble the King of Beasts physically, but not at all in temperament. The little fellows (10 inches in height, weighing 12 pounds or less) are sprightly and affectionate house pets. Color can be gray, white-cream, or black. (Toy: 2)

LUMBERING: having an awkward gait.

M

MAIDEN: an unmated bitch.

MALAMUTE: see *Alaskan Malamute*.

MALINOIS: see *Belgian Malinois*.

MALTESE: A tiny, snow-white dog whose ancestry goes back to ancient Greece and Rome, and whose picture was painted by such noted English portraitists as Sir Joshua Reynolds and Sir Edwin Landseer, the Maltese has been a lapdog from then to now. Its long, silky, straight coat requires considerable gooming; its whims need to be indulged; and it needs careful feeding and moderate exercise. A lively and spirited pet, the Maltese enjoys being the center of attention. Preferred weight is from 4 to 6 pounds, with a maximum height of 5 inches. (Toy: 1–2–3–4)

Maltese

MAMMARY GLANDS (breasts): Most bitches have five breasts on each side of the abdomen. During pregnancy the mammary glands enlarge and secrete milk to feed the expected litter. This enlargement can also occur during the two months following a heat period, even if the bitch has not been bred. The mammary glands often develop cysts and tumors (benign or malignant); thus any lump in the breast should be investigated promptly by a veterinarian. (See also *false pregnancy*.)

Manchester Terrier

MANCHESTER TERRIER: This graceful, sleek dog with its short, glossy coat long ago hunted rats and coursed rabbits in England. The present breed stems from a nineteenth-century cross between a Whippet bitch and a renowned ratter of indeterminate ancestry. For the nonathletic, fastidious dog owner, it is an ideal house pet —requiring little exercise, shedding minimally, and not prone to "doggy" odors. The dog, with its distinctive rich tan markings on an ebony-black coat, can range in height from 14 to 16 inches and in weight from 12 to 22 pounds. White markings of one-half inch or more in length are disqualifying faults in the show ring. (Terrier: 1–2–3–4)

MANCHESTER TOY TERRIER: see *English Toy Terrier.*

MANE: long hair falling from the top and sides of neck.

MANGE (Scabies): a worldwide, contagious, parasitic skin disease caused by a mite (*Sarcoptes scabiei var. canis)*. The mites live in the horny layers of the epidermis and sometimes burrow into the deeper layers of the skin. They may be shed together with scales and hair, landing on furniture, kennel floors, etc., where they can infect a new host.

Signs include intense itching, baldness, and thickening of the skin due to self-inflicted injuries. Mange usually starts at the margins of the ears or around the tail, and if not treated, it can spread over the entire body. Dogs of all ages may be affected, but the disease is most severe in young puppies. Treatment includes dipping and the application of suitable chemicals, and is usually effective within a few weeks. In long-haired dogs, it may be necessary to shave the entire coat. During treatment the dog should be isolated so that it does not infect other animals. The premises must be thoroughly scrubbed, cleaned, and disinfected. Sarcoptic mange can infect people, but the disease is usually mild and responds rapidly to appropriate treatment.

Demodectic mange (red mange or follicular mange) is a disease of the skin associated with the presence of a mite (*demodex canis*) in the deep parts of the hair follicles. It is commonly seen in young dogs of the short-haired breeds (Dachshunds, Boston Terrier, etc.) where it appears as small, hairless areas on the face and nose. Many facts about demodectic mange are still unknown, and much research is necessary. Some dogs respond to treatment within a few weeks, while other cases are refractory even after intensive efforts.

MANTLE: a coat on the back, shoulders, and sides of a darker shade than the rest of the coat.

MARBLED: having coloring that is mottled.

MAREMMA ITALIAN SHEEPDOG: Well-known in Italy in the Abruzzi and Tuscany areas, this dog is less familiar elsewhere, though specimens of the breed began to appear in England in the 1930's. A large, white dog (23 to 29 inches tall and weighing from

Maremma Italian Sheepdog

55 to 100 pounds), with a bearlike head and a soft coat of medium length, the Maremma resembles a refined version of the more familiar Great Pyrenees. (Working: 2)

MASTER: leader of a hunt.

Mastiff

MASTIFF: A term once used to describe any large dog, "massive" is the word that best fits this ancient breed, aptly registered as the Old English Mastiff in Canada. Despite having been favored for bull and bear baiting in the days of Henry VIII in England, and despite its awe-inspiring appearance, the dog is gentle, affectionate, calm, and an excellent house pet. Breed standards call for dogs to be a minimum of 30 inches high at the shoulders; bitches should be a minimum of 27½ inches, with no upper limit set. Weight is in proportion and can be as much as 185 pounds. The short, coarse coat can be apricot, dark fawn-brindle, or silver-fawn. The muzzle, nose, area around the eyes, and ears must be dark in color, with black preferred. (Working: 1–2–3)

MATCH SHOW: an informal dog show at which championship points are not awarded and entries are usually not made in advance.

MATING: A male dog is ready to mate when it is one year old and can continue to breed until it is ten years or more. However, if not mated by its fifth year, the male will still have sexual instincts but may lack sufficient technique. It is usually advisable to mate a young stud to an experienced brood bitch, and vice versa. The bitch should not be mated before her second heat. (See also *breeding*.)

Mating should take place in a quiet area familiar to the stud dog. Neither dog nor bitch should be fed for several hours prior to mating. Before breeding, the stud and bitch should be introduced to each other on leash, and should be allowed time to become acquainted. If the bitch is young or nervous, it may be necessary for the handler to apply a light tape muzzle to prevent injury to the stud. Within a few minutes a receptive bitch will swish her tail to one side and stand still. The stud will mount her and penetrate. They may then remain tied together for a period of five to thirty minutes or longer. The bitch should be held quietly in position so as not to injure the stud dog. A bitch can conceive even though an actual tie does not accur. Frequently, the stud will dismount once a tie is established and will stand facing away from the bitch. After the tie is broken, the stud and bitch should be kenneled and allowed to rest. Fresh drinking water should be made available to both.

MEDICATION: Before administering any medication, it is important to read carefully the instructions on the label, including all the fine print.

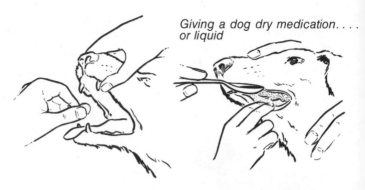

Giving a dog dry medication. . . . or liquid

Liquid medicines are best given with a spoon or small bottle. Raise the dog's head and gently pull the lips away from the back teeth to form a pocket. When the liquid is poured slowly into the pocket, it will pass behind the teeth and go directly into the gullet. To induce rapid swallowing, it is sometimes necessary to hold the dog's nose. This method avoids the danger that the medicine will "go the wrong way" into the trachea or lungs. In snappy dogs this method can be used together with a tape muzzle.

Tablets and capsules may be crushed and mixed with strong-smelling food. If the dog is not eating, or is too smart for this method, the dose must be given by hand. Raise the head and open the mouth by pressing the lips between the upper and lower back teeth. Using your fingers or a forceps, place the tablet behind the bump of the tongue, pull the tongue out slightly, and allow the mouth to close.

MERLE: a mixture of blue, gray, white, and black flecks of color on a dog's coat. Collies, Shetland Sheepdogs, and Cardigan Welsh Corgis are often so marked.

MEXICAN HAIRLESS: apparently of African origin, the Mexican Hairless is built like a terrier, with long legs and prick ears, and is indeed hairless except for a permissible tuft on the crown of its head and at the end of its long tail. Its skin can be any color, solid or patched; its height is about 11 inches, and its weight about 11 pounds. The breed, loving and lively, but not likely to thrive where it is cold and damp, vocalizes by crying instead of barking. (Toy: 3)

Mexican Hairless

MEXICO: All shows and trials are held under rules established by the Asociacion Canofila Mexicana, Zacatecas 229-Desp. 318, Mexico 7, D.F.

MINIATURE PINSCHER: A trim little dog, which has been in existence for several centuries in its native Germany and in the Scandinavian countries, the Miniature Pinscher has such poise and self-confidence that it seems much larger than it really is—10 to 12½ inches at the withers and weighing from 8 to 10 pounds. A stylish dog, the Miniature Pinscher moves with a characteristic high-stepping hackney-pony gait, a movement that is faulted in most breeds. Its short, sleek coat always looks well-groomed; it is loyal to home and family and an excellent watchdog. Its coat can be solid red or stag red; black with clearly defined tan or rust-red markings; or solid brown or chocolate with rust or yellow markings. Areas of white exceeding one-half inch in length on the feet or forechest are considered a disqualification. (Toy: 1–2–3–4)

Miniature Schnauzer

Miniature Pinscher

MINIATURE SCHNAUZER: Classified as a separate breed in the United States and Canada, the Miniature Schnauzer is a very much smaller edition (12–14 inches high at the shoulder) of the *Standard Schnauzer*, possessing the same square, rugged, Terrier-like build with a bold, active disposition. Despite his small size, he should never be so refined as to appear delicate or toyish. The Miniature has the same harsh, wiry coat, beard, prominent eyebrows, and furnishings of the larger Schnauzers but more variation of coloring is acceptable. In addition to the salt and pepper or pure black colors, black and silver, following the salt and pepper pattern, is permitted as is tan shading with the salt and pepper coloring. As with the other Schnauzer breeds, the ears are either cropped with pointed tips or if uncropped, the small, V-shaped ears fold close to the head. The docked tail is carried erect and should be long enough to be seen over the topline when the dog is in proper coat.

Though primarily developed as a ratter and a stable dog from a cross of the Affenpinscher and small Standard Schnauzers, the Miniature is tremendously popular today as a family pet and watch dog. (Terrier: 1–3; Utility: 2–4)

MISCELLANEOUS CLASS: In the United States this is a class at shows for dogs of certain breeds specified by the board of directors of the American Kennel Club for which no regular classification exists. All Miscellaneous Breeds are shown together in one class at any given show. Dogs of Miscellaneous Breeds cannot earn championship points, nor can they compete in group competitions. These breeds are eligible to compete in obedience and tracking trials and can earn obedience degrees.

MISMARKED: having a color pattern that does not conform to the breed standard.

MODELING: see *careers for dogs*.

MONGREL: any dog whose parents were of mixed breed, or purebreds of two different breeds. Dogs of a mixed heritage are not eligible for kennel club registration, nor can they be entered in events sanctioned by a kennel club. In a few countries mongrels can compete in obedience trials.

MONORCHIDISM: a condition in an adult male dog in which one testicle is abnormally retained in the abdominal cavity and the other has descended normally into the scrotum. Such dogs *can* breed, but they are barred from competition at AKC shows. Some geneticists believe the trait is hereditary. (See also *cryptorchidism*.)

MOULTING: see *shedding*.

MOUNTAIN DOGS: Contrary to legend, no St. Bernard or other so-called Mountain Dog ever carried a keg of liquid, spirituous or otherwise, around its neck. More than two hundred years ago, however, hospice monks used these animals to test the newly fallen snow each morning to determine if a path through the mountains was navigable. Later they were (and still are) used as rescue dogs since their keen nose enables them to locate luckless skiers or climbers who may be buried beneath a drift following an avalanche or fall. Nowadays German Shepherds are being used increasingly for rescue work.

A proud young owner gives final instructions before her Pyrenean Mountain Dog enters the British show ring.

Large Munsterlander

MUNSTERLANDER (Large): A gundog that is steady on point and a good retriever either on land or in water, this dog is medium-sized (from 23 to 25 inches tall) and resembles a Setter in build and coat quality, though its head is quite Spaniellike. Its slightly wavy, white coat is heavily marked with black ticking, and it has a black head and large black body patches. The dog has plenty of perserverance and stamina in the field, and is a likeable, responsive house pet as well. (Gundog: 2)

Small Munsterlander

MUNSTERLANDER (Small): The chief differences between this breed (also known as the Moorland Spaniel) and its larger relative are that it is both smaller (17 to 22 inches tall) and more lightly built and that its coat is brown and white. Neither color necessarily predominates, though the head is usually brown. The second color appears as patches rather than as a blanket ticking. Tan markings over the eyes and on the muzzle are allowed. (Gundog: 2; Sporting Gundog: 2)

MUSIC: the baying of hounds.

MUSIC, Response to: Despite tales to the contrary, dogs are not music lovers and can be lulled to sleep as easily by rock music as by a Brahms symphony. Nonetheless, they respond actively to variations in a human voice: an enthusiastic greeting will usually elicit a joyous, tail-wagging response; a harsh reprimand, a look of total dejection.

MUZZLE: the part of a dog's head from the eyes forward.

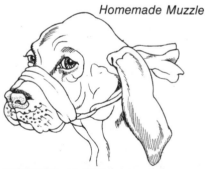

Homemade Muzzle

MUZZLES: Used to prevent dogs from biting, muzzles are of two types: wire or leather devices manufactured and sold for use on vicious or overaggressive animals; and home-made muzzles made from a soft bandage or pliable belt, used while examining an injured dog. A noose is formed and placed over the dog's nose and a knot is tied beneath the dog's jaws. The loose ends of the muzzle are tied firmly behind the ears.

N

NAILS: horny outgrowths on the toes. Nails should be inspected regularly, and if overgrown, they must be clipped or filed back in order to prevent lameness or deformity of the feet. The nails on the dewclaws (especially those of the hind legs of Briards and similar breeds) tend to curl and grow into the flesh if proper care is not taken. The nails of nursing puppies grow very rapidly and should be clipped with a pair of scissors to prevent injury to the mother's breasts. To clip nails, an animal nail clipper is needed (scissors are unsatisfactory for adult dogs). Hold the foot to the light so that the blood vessels in light-colored nails can be seen, and remove only the overhanging, horny parts of the nail. With black nails, the "quick," or outer limit of the blood vessels, cannot be seen, so one must clip small sections of the nail at a time until the brittle dried part of the nail is removed. To do a perfect job, smooth the rough edges with a coarse metal file.

NEOPLASM: see *tumors*.

NEPHRITIS: see *kidney diseases*.

NEW BREEDS: From time to time a new breed is recognized by a national kennel club for breeding and competition at shows, but usually the breed is actually an "old" breed that simply had not yet been

The Gallic Bichon Frise is now recognized in America.

established in a particular country. All kennel clubs take a dim view of newly invented breeds since it takes generations to stabilize them.

Newfoundland

NEWFOUNDLAND: A good-natured, gentle dog of massive size, the Newfoundland gained fame in its native land as a superb water dog. With its tremendous strength, slightly oily, water-resistant coat, and large webbed feet, the Newfoundland is well equipped for rescue work at sea.

In addition to its duties as a water dog, the Newfoundland can be trained to pull carts and carry loads on its back. In the home the Newfoundland is an obedient and intelligent companion and a dependable guardian of both home and children.

Average height for the breed is from 26 to 28 inches; weight ranges from 120 to 150 pounds. The dog is typically dull jet-black in color, sometimes with small white markings on the chest, feet, or tail. Other colors are permitted, but the black-and-white (Landseer) variety or a bronze color is encouraged. (Working: 1–2–3; Nonsporting: 4)

NEW ZEALAND KENNEL CLUB: Affiliated with the Kennel Club of England, this organization was founded nearly ninety years ago and welcomes judges from overseas at its shows and field trials. It sets its own rules, which closely parallel the British system of Challenge Certificates, and takes particular pride in the work it has done to increase the popularity of working Sheepdogs that are indigenous, for the most part, to Australasia. Address: P.O. Box 523, Wellington 1, New Zealand.

NIGHT BLINDNESS: Also called progressive retinal atrophy, this disease appears to be hereditary in certain breeds.

NONSLIP RETRIEVER: a dog that stays at heel, marks the fall of game, and retrieves it on command.

Norfolk Terrier

NORFOLK TERRIER: In 1964 the English Kennel Club gave permission to divide the erect and the button-ear varieties of the Norwich Terrier into two separate breeds. Those with erect ears remained classified as Norwich Terriers, and the button-ear variety became designated as Norfolk Terriers. In the United States and Canada the two varieties remain classified as a single breed, the Norwich Terrier. The Norfolk Terrier differs from the parent breed in ear carriage only, and all other characteristics of the Norwich Terrier have been retained. (Terrier: 2)

NORWAY: For information, write the Norsk Kennel Club, Bjorn Farmannsgate 16, North Oslo 2.

Norwegian Buhund

Norwegian Elkhound

NORWEGIAN BUHUND: Known for centuries in Norway, the Buhund wasn't recognized until 1943 by the English Kennel Club and has yet to be recognized by the American Kennel Club. A Spitz type and a good guard dog and companion, the Buhund stands about 17 inches high and has a long topcoat that is heavy and hard and a soft, thick undercoat. Preferred colors are black, medium red, and wheaten. A white blaze, collar around the neck, or spot on the chest or feet is allowed. Like most members of the Spitz family, this dog has a high-set, thick tail that it carries curled over its back. (Working: 2)

NORWEGIAN ELKHOUND: Archaeological findings indicate that this stocky, powerful hunter of Scandinavia possibly existed in the Stone Age, and it is noted in the history of the breed that the Elkhound hunted bear for its Viking masters before the days when it was used to hunt European elk. A highly intelligent, responsive dog, the Norwegian Elkhound has been adapted to a variety of other uses, which include serving as a sled dog, a useful farm dog, and a guardian of the home and family. It is a striking-looking dog of medium size (19¼ to 20½ inches high), whose very dense, straight coat is gray in color with the ends of the hairs tipped with black. Any marked deviation from the gray coloring is considered to be a disqualifying fault in the show ring. In England these dogs are registered simply as Elkhounds. (Hound: 1–2–3–4)

NORWICH TERRIER: An independent, small, robust dog with a pointed foxy muzzle and a hard, wiry coat that is typically red in color but may be black and tan or grizzle, the Norwich Terrier was developed to be a game-hunting dog and a fearless ratter. The Norwich Terrier, originally called the Jones Terrier when first imported to the United States after World War I, is described in its breed standard as being a "perfect demon yet not quarrelsome and of a lovable disposition." The small size of the Norwich (10 inches at the withers, and from 11 to 12 pounds), its cleanliness, and its tidy coat that needs little grooming are qualities that, combined with an alert, active disposition, have made this dog increasingly popular as a house pet. (See also *Norfolk Terrier*.) (Terrier: 1–2–3)

NOSE: the ability to detect by scent. Dogs find and follow their quarry chiefly with their noses, and to a lesser extent with their ears. With the exception of the sight hounds, dogs hunt very little with their eyes (although at night dogs see better than humans do). It has been said that a dog's sense of smell is its mind, and when one realizes that a dog can detect the presence of one drop of blood in five quarts of water, one begins to appreciate the truth of this statement. Thus, exercises in scent discrimination are an important part of advanced obedience training courses.

Of many different scents that impress themselves on his olfactory cells, this German Shorthaired Pointer will infallibly select the one he is directed to by his owner, and follow it unswervingly.

NOVA SCOTIA DUCK TOLLING DOG: Somewhere in the past of this fox-red dog is the Chesapeake Bay Retriever, and perhaps a little Golden Retriever as well. What it does is thrash around and make a ruckus at the water's edge sufficient to arouse the curiosity of ducks swimming offshore. It is a matter of "curiosity killed the duck," because when the ducks swim in close enough to investigate, there is usually a concealed hunter within easy range. In keeping with its heritage, the dog winds up the job by retrieving the birds. The breed averages 20½ inches tall at the shoulder and 50 pounds in weight. (Sporting: 3)

NURSING BITCH: After delivery, bitches will settle down and nurse their puppies for two to three weeks without help from the owner. Some nervous bitches (especially after the first litter) may require a mild tranquilizer for a few days. While nursing, a bitch must be provided with a suitable box filled with soft, clean bedding, such as old towels, shredded newspapers, or hay. She must be kept in a quiet place, separated from other dogs, and whenever possible, close to the sight or sound of the owner. Visits by strangers should be avoided because they may cause the bitch to become nervous and abandon her puppies.

A nursing bitch requires a liberal diet rich in proteins, calcium, and milk products. Special supplements for large litters are available, but their use must be supervised by a veterinarian in order to avoid an unbalanced ratio. One meal in the morning and one at night is recommended; milk may be given in between, and water should be available at all times.

During the first week a bitch will leave her puppies only long enough to evacuate. Later she should be encouraged to take short periods of rest and exercise.

Weaning begins three to four weeks after the birth of the pups and should be completed by six weeks. Normally, the milk will begin to dry up at six weeks. At this time the owner must watch carefully for signs of redness or engorgement of the breast. If engorgement should occur, a small amount of milk may be withdrawn, or the puppies allowed to nurse for a short period after their evening meal.

OBEDIENCE TRAINING: Training should begin when a puppy arrives in your home. A two- or three-month pup can be taught the essentials: housebreaking; where it is to sleep each night; walking with a leash attached, perhaps even to sit and stay on command.

At four to eight months of age (authorities differ on this) formal training should begin. The owner has several choices:

1. He can train the dog himself, aided by a vast number of books and training manuals.

2. There are professional trainers, some of whom take the dog away for boarding and a training course, some of whom come to one's home to instruct both dog and owner.

3. There are a growing number of schools and obedience-training clubs that offer regular classes for both puppies and mature dogs.

Whatever training method is chosen, there are a few general and all-important rules to follow:

1. The owner needs to be trained as well as the dog.

Members of an Obedience Training Club practice heeling.

Learning to sit patiently and stay in position while the owner

2. Consistency and patience are absolute essentials in an owner.

3. There is no need, *ever,* to shout at or physically punish a recalcitrant animal. Commands should be given in a firm but pleasant tone of voice.

4. Commands should be simple and almost always of one word. Typical examples are: Sit! Stay! Come! Down!

5. A command, once chosen, should never be changed. Thus, if the command for misbehavior is "NO!" it should never be changed

is out of sight is one of the basics of obedience training.

to "Stop That!" or "Bad Dog!" Changing commands will only produce a confused dog.

6. Do not expect a dog to obey a command the fifth or fiftieth time it is given. If your patience is wearing thin, stop the training session and begin again the following day.

7. Do not train a dog immediately after it has been fed.

8. When the dog does something right, praise it lavishly.

9. Each session should end on an upbeat note, with the dog in high spirits and convinced of the brilliance of its accomplishments.

Basic training: The tools needed are a training collar (see *collars*), a leash at least six feet in length, and a long clothesline.

Heeling: Keep the dog on your left side, with its leash bunched up in your right hand. Use your left hand for corrections, which are made with sharp, quick jerks on the leash. When corrections are not needed, the leash should always be loose. Use voice commands, and keep the dog's attention at all times. Step forward briskly and give the commnd "Heel!" The dog's head and shoulders should be on a line with your left leg. If the dog forges ahead or lags behind, a jerk on the leash will tighten the collar and quickly bring it into its proper position.

1. Heeling: *The leash is held loosely in the trainer's right hand, but the Poodle is beginning to lag behind.*

2. Heeling: *A quick tug on the leash brings pressure on the dog's neck and brings him up to the correct heeling position.*

Unless corrected, dogs will form a habit of sitting in front of the owner or behind him, or at an angle. Here the trainer teaches her Poodle the correct Sit—close to her left leg and parallel to it.

The Sit: This is taught with the dog at heel position. When you give the command "Sit!" pull the lead up sharply with your right hand while, simultaneously you force the dog's rump down with your left hand. When the dog sits, relax the pressures immediately and warmly praise the dog. The sit is combined with heeling so that the dog learns to sit every time you halt.

Note how both hands are used to keep the Poodle in a stationary position. Later, in the show ring, the dog will stand by himself while the show judge examines him.

The Stand: With the dog at your side in a sitting position, stride forward a few paces, giving the command "Heel!" and then, a few steps farther on, the second command, "Stand!" With your right hand, hold the leash tight near the collar, keeping the dog's head up. Place your left hand, palm down, under the dog's stomach, preventing it from moving its hind legs. (An alternative method is to loop the lead under the dog's body, exerting an upward pressure that will prevent it from moving or lying down.)

1. The Recall: *With the dog sitting, at the end of the lead, the owner calls the Poodle's name and gives the command: "Roger! Come!"*

2. The Recall: *As the dog approaches, the trainer holds the lead loosely but draws it in. If the Poodle lags, a quick tightening of the leash will quickly put him back on the proper course.*

3. The Recall: *When the dog is directly in front of the trainer it sits at once. In later training, the distance between dog and handler is increased by a clothesline tied to the lead until, finally, the exercise is done off lead.*

1. The Come-to-heel or Finish: *With the dog sitting in front of the owner the command "Heel!" is given. As the Poodle starts to move, the trainer guides it by moving the leash in an arc with the left hand.*

158

2. The Finish: *As the trainer completes the arc, the Poodle is gently guided to her left side.*

3. The Finish: *Once the dog has made the complete turn, the command "Sit!" is given. When the dog obeys, pressure on the leash is relaxed. The exercise completed, the dog is warmly praised.*

159

1. The Down or Drop: *With the dog at the end of the lead, the command "Come!" is given, followed by the command "Down!" If the Poodle keeps advancing, the trainer steps down smartly on the leash, which is simultaneously tightened with the right hand.*

2. The Drop: *Pressure on the lead is gradually increased until the Poodle approaches the desired position. Once he is Down and stays Down, the dog is praised lavishly.*

160

3. The Drop: *An alternate method of teaching the Down command is to pull the front legs out with the left hand while pushing down on the hindquarters with the right.*

4. The Drop: *The Poodle is now in the proper Down position. Soon he will be promptly obeying the vocal command off lead and without physical interference by the trainer.*

Once a dog has mastered these basics, it is ready for more advanced training. But it should have mastered them thoroughly. Practice periods should be short—not more than ten minutes—but held twice a day if possible. When teaching a new exercise, always review the ones the dog is already familiar with. Corrections must be made quickly, and praise must immediately follow a properly executed exercise. Food rewards are used by some trainers, others do not approve of this tactic.

While techniques and exercise in advanced training vary somewhat from country to country, the end achieved is always the same.

Most intermediate exercises teach a dog to heel off lead; to sit with a group of dogs for three minutes while the owner is out of sight; to stay down under the same conditions for five minutes; to drop instantly on recall; to go over a broad jump; and to retrieve objects on flat ground or over hurdles.

Advanced obedience-training routines include, among others, exercises in scent discrimination, in which the dog selects from many objects the one bearing its owner's scent; obeying commands by hand

Teaching a dog to retrieve over a hurdle. With the Poodle on lead and at her side, the trainer is walking him over a low hurdle to show what is expected.

162

Jumping over several low spaced-out hurdles is another of the intermediate obedience exercises.

The height of the hurdle is gradually increased. By this time the Poodle is sent by command over the hurdle, finds a dumbbell which has been tossed over by the trainer, recrosses the hurdle and sits in front of the trainer offering her the retrieved object.

The broad jump on command. Once the barrier has been crossed, the dog will return to the trainer and sit facing her, awaiting the come-to-heel command which completes the exercise.

signal only; "going out" a considerable distance from the owner, stopping and sitting on command, and then returning over a specifically designated obstacle or hurdle; picking up and following a scent for tracking; standing for examination for at least three minutes; plus other postgraduate routines.

The object of obedience training is not to teach a dog "tricks."

Among other things, such training can save the dog's life, for a dog that stays at its owner's side will not rush off into the path of oncoming vehicles, while one who drops instantly on recall can be kept out of all sorts of trouble.

Above all, as innumerable owners have discovered, a well-trained dog is a joy to own, while an unruly one is a source of endless headaches.

164

Many large breeds enjoy greeting children and adults with excessive enthusiasm. One way to break this habit is to bring a knee up sharply against the dog's chest while at the same time giving some such command as "Off!" Repeated enough times, the dog will find some less physical type of welcome.

One final word: some breeds are far easier to train than others, but even the most stubborn of breeds will eventually learn their lessons if, and only if, the trainer has the patience required.

Retrieving game birds (live or wooden) is just one of the exercises in advanced training which owners and dogs alike find highly gratifying.

OBESITY (gross overweight): a common condition in pet dogs. If not corrected, it can lead to serious complications such as heart disease, strain on the back and legs, or lack of fertility. The most common cause is overindulgence by owners—overfeeding (especially snacks between meals) or an improperly balanced diet. Other causes include insufficient exercise, thyroid or other hormonal disorders, and diabetes. If a dog is obese, it should be examined by a veterinarian whose instructions should be carried out faithfully.

OCCIPUT: the upper back point of the skull.

OLD ENGLISH MASTIFF: see *mastiff*.

Old English Sheepdog

OLD ENGLISH SHEEPDOG: This big charmer has steadily grown in popularity over the years in many lands; in the United States its ascent has been dramatic. Once a guardian of flocks and later used to drive sheep to market, it is today a house pet that does well in obedience competitions and excels in the show ring. Also called the Bobtail (when it is two or three days old the tail is removed at the first

joint), it is sturdy and even-tempered, affectionate, and something of a stay-at-home. Beneath the hair covering its face, one finds liquid, loving eyes, and its ambling gait is deceptive, for it conceals great musculature. Dogs range from 21 to 25 inches in height, bitches are a bit less; and compactness of body is more important than weight. The dog needs considerable brushing since its coat (gray, blue, or grizzle with white markings, or the reverse) has a tendency to mat. (Working: 1–2–3–4)

OPEN BITCH: a bitch that can be bred.

OPEN CLASS: in dog shows, generally a division in which dogs of the same breed (six months or over) may enter.

OTTERHOUND: As the pollution of British streams increased, fish died and the otters left, an environmental problem that drastically affected the Otterhound, whose job for centuries was to track the otter to its "home." This big, web-footed descendant of the bloodhound is a superb water dog with a mild and gentle disposition, but it is, apparently, too specialized to gain popularity in the United

Otterhound

States. The dogs range from 22 to 27 inches in height and average around 75 pounds for bitches, 90 for males. The dog's coat, crisp and water-repellent, is typically a

Otter Tail

sandy color with somewhat defined black-and-tan markings. (Hound: 1–2–3)

OTTER TAIL: a round tail, tapering from a thick root, with the hair parted on the underside.

OUT AT SHOULDERS: shoulder blades that jut out loosely from the body.

OUT OF COAT: coat out of condition, usually during period of shedding.

OVERSHOT: having an upper jaw in which the front teeth overlap and do not touch the front teeth in the lower jaw when the dog's mouth is closed.

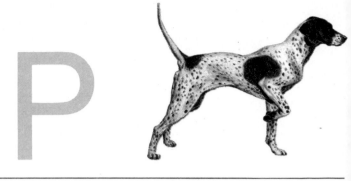

P

PACE: a gait like that of a horse which is a "pacer": the legs on one side of the body advance together, alternating with the two legs on the other side, instead of the more common trot in which the foreleg and the hind leg on the opposite side move forward in unison.

PACK: a number of hounds maintained together in one kennel. Depending on the type of hound, the kind of quarry it is best suited for following, and the terrain for the hunt, the hounds are followed by riders on horseback or hunters on foot. In England, the stronghold of

Trotting, rather than pacing a dog, for a show judge's approval.

A large pack of hounds joyously set out on a hunt.

pack hunting, the sport extends roughly from mid-fall to early spring, except for draghounds, which are run all year round, and Otterhounds, which hunt in summer.

PAD: the tough-skinned cushion on the sole of a dog's foot.

PADDLING: a gait in which the forefeet move too wide and are likely to turn out as they come up at the end of each step.

PAKISTAN: Canine activities in this land that spawned many of the sleek gaze-hounds of centuries past are regulated by the Kennel Club of Pakistan, Fortress Stadium, Lahore, West Pakistan.

PANTING: Evaporation of perspiration in a dog takes place principally through panting. Once the body has sufficiently cooled, the panting stops.

PAPER PADS: flat-feet, caused by thin or inadequately cushioned pads.

Paper Foot

PAPILLON: This dainty and lively Toy Spaniel, a palace pet of Marie Antoinette's, was probably bred originally in Spain and Italy despite its French name, meaning "butterfly," which describes its large, beautifully fringed ears. The ears may be either erect or drooping, but the button ear, in the variety known as the phalene, must be

169

Papillon

carried completely down. An elegant, fine-boned dog, the Papillon carries a profuse, long, silky, straight coat that forms a heavy frill on the chest and a heavy, long plume on the tail. Coat color is basically white with patches of any color other than liver. Show-ring disqualifications for the breed are a height in excess of 12 inches and a coat that is a solid color, is all white, has white around the eyes or on the ears, has no white, or is a liver color. The Papillon is a perky house pet and has proved itself to be extremely competent in the obedience ring. (Toy: 1–2–3–4)

PARALYSIS: the inability of a muscle to function normally due to disease of the nerve supply. The nerve may be injured by a virus (e.g., canine distemper) or by an accident. Paralysis may be local, affecting a single nerve (the radial nerve of the front leg, for example), or it may be generalized, involving all the nerves in the spinal cord, as in the paralysis of the hind legs so frequently seen in Dachshunds.

PARTI-COLORED: having a coat that has patches of two or more colors.

PASTERN: the foreleg between the wrist (carpus) and the toes.

PEDIGREE: a written record, backed by documentary proof, of a dog's ancestry. Pedigrees usually cover at least three generations and are supplied to the purchaser of a purebred animal by the breeder or at other points of sale. The sire and dam are first shown, then the grandparents, etc., with the credentials— Champion or Field Champion —indicated. Other data relevant to the puppy being purchased is included.

Pekingese

PEKINGESE: An ancient and once sacred Chinese breed, this dog's recorded history goes back to the eighth-century Tang dynasty. Representatives of the breed were variously known as lion dogs, sun dogs (whose coats were red-gold), and sleeve dogs—for those small enough to be carried around the palace up a sleeve. The dogs made their way to the Western world in 1860 after the British sacked the Imperial Palace in Peking. Many of the residents of the household killed their dogs and then committed suicide just before the attack, but four dogs, one of which was later given to Queen Victoria, were found by the looters.

Despite its size—weight, 5 to 14 pounds, and 10 to 11 inches tall —the dog is dignified, fearless, and has great stamina. It has long

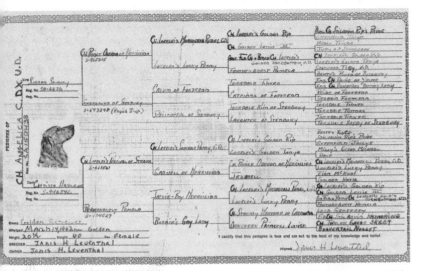

Typical pedigree showing five generations of Golden Retrievers

enjoyed great and deserved popularity. Its profuse, long, straight, flat coat can be any color, with black on the muzzle and around the eyes being desired. (Toy: 1–2–3–4)

PEMBROKE WELSH CORGI: A breed probably brought to Wales by Flemish weavers whom Henry I persuaded to come to England in 1107, this is an alert, intelligent working farm dog. Though it has undoubtedly been crossed often with its cousin, the Cardigan Welsh Corgi, the Pembroke is a distinct breed with its own characteristics: shorter body, lighter bones,

Pembroke Welsh Corgi

straighter front legs, smaller, more pointed ears, and a very short tail. A small dog (10 to 12 inches tall and weighing not more than 30 pounds) and foxlike in appearance, it is an affectionate, protective companion. Its medium-length coat can be black and tan, fawn, red, or sable, with or without white markings. (Working: 1–2–3–4)

PEOPLE'S DISPENSARY FOR SICK ANIMALS: Founded in London in 1917 to provide free care to sick pets whose owners couldn't afford to pay a veterinarian, the service continues to provide such assistance in more than two hundred centers in the United Kingdom. In addition, ambulance facilities, hospitals for critical cases, shelters for stray cats and dogs, and instructions in the care of sick and injured animals are included in the services of the organization, which is maintained by voluntary contributions.

171

PERSPIRATION: Dogs perspire chiefly through their footpads, tongue, and mouth. (See also *panting*.)

Pharaoh Hound

PHARAOH HOUND: Perhaps originally developed by the rulers of ancient Egypt to hunt gazelles, this dog is a member of the Greyhound family and, like its relatives, is noted primarily for speed. Despite the Pharaoh Hound's erect ears, it is a sight hound and depends very little on its sense of hearing. This medium-sized dog—22 to 25 inches high—with its short, shining coat of chestnut or rich tan with white markings, is bright, lively, and loving, and needs lots of exercise. White coloration must be confined to tail tip, chest, toes, and a thin line in the middle of the face. (Hound: 2)

PIED: having sizable patches of two or more colors on the coat. Also called *piebald*.

PIGEON BREAST: a chest with a short, protruding breastbone.

PINCER BITE: when the tips of upper and lower teeth meet, as in a level bite.

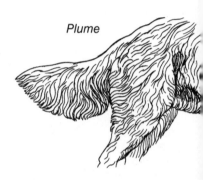

Plume

PLUME: a long "feather" or fringe of hair on the underside of the tail.

PNEUMONIA: an inflammation of the lungs. It may be caused by virus, bacteria, or fungi. It is always serious because it reduces the amount of air a dog can breathe. Most cases of pneumonia respond well to the newer antibiotics and careful nursing.

POINT: the rigid stance of a hunting dog, indicating that game is close, and with the nose in the direction where it hides.

Pharaoh Hounds today look much as they did in ancient Egypt.

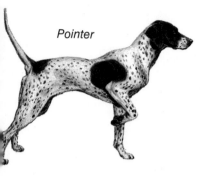
Pointer

POINTER: the recorded history of this remarkable gundog goes back to about 1650 in England, where the breed took to the field to locate hares, which were then hunted down by Greyhounds. Over the years, it has been crossed and recrossed with Pointers from other countries and with Setters of various kinds to produce a hardworking and noble bird dog, combining grace, courage, and stamina. It is adaptable enough to work at field trials with handlers unfamiliar to it and develops hunting instincts when it is very young —sometimes pointing at two months of age. Its short coat (solid black or white with liver, lemon, orange, or black) is trim and clean in home or kennel. Dogs range in size from 23 to 28 inches tall and in weight from 45 to 75 pounds. (Sporting 1–3; Gundog: 2–4)

Classic posture of a Gundog in the field.

*Pointing
Wirehaired Griffon*

POINTING WIRE-HAIRED GRIF-FON: While not a fast working dog, this efficient, medium-sized animal has a fine nose, is a good retriever, and excels as a hunter of pheasants and waterfowl. Once called the *Korthals Griffon* (after its breeder, Eduard Korthals) the dog emerged more than a century ago in France, and was introduced to the British scene some nine decades ago. Height of the male ranges from 21 to 23½ inches, and the dog has a somewhat stockier body than other Pointers. Its coat is short and bristly, with a soft undercoat and the tail is traditionally docked. Black is taboo as a color, which is generally grey mixed with chestnut. The dog is known in the U.S. as the Wire-Haired Pointing Griffon. (Sporting: 1; Gun Dog: 2)

POISONS, CHEMICAL: If poisoning is suspected, immediate professional treatment is necessary to prevent complications or even death. Whenever possible, the package containing the suspected chemical should be saved and given to the veterinarian, so that proper antidotes may be administered as soon as possible. As a first-aid measure or in remote areas the owner may often save a dog's life by inducing vomiting. This can be accomplished by giving the dog large quantities of salt water (four tablespoons of salt in one pint of water).

Most accidental poisonings can be prevented if the owner is aware of the following and takes the necessary precautions.

1. *Lead* is present in the paint scrapings of older houses. It causes chronic disease in older dogs and acute disturbances in puppies.

2. *Insecticides,* especially flea dips used too frequently or in excessive concentrations, can be absorbed through the skin and lead to cumulative poisoning.

3. *Metaldehyde* used as a fuel or in slug and snail poisons can cause severe muscle tremors.

4. *Strychnine* is present in many rat poisons.

5. *Warfarin* is present in rat poisons. Although supposedly safe for use around dogs, it can cause severe internal bleeding if ingested in small quantities over a prolonged period.

6. *Ethylene glycol* (antifreeze) can cause acute symptoms and death within one to three days.

7. *Thallium* or *arsenic* may be present in ant killers and rat poisons.

Most weed killers and plant sprays contain chemicals that may be toxic to susceptible dogs —especially puppies.

POISONS, PLANT: While most animals, including house pets, appear to avoid eating poisonous plants instinctively, some of them, particularly puppies, may at one

TABLE OF COMMON POISONOUS PLANTS*

PLANT	TOXIC PART
COMMON LILIES: amaryllis, daffodil, tulip; jonquil, narcissus, death camas, autumn crocus, star-of-Bethlehem, lily of the valley, others.	bulbs mostly
TROPICAL POTTED ORNAMENTALS: caladium, philodendron, dumb-cane (*Dieffenbachia*), elephant ear and similar common house plants.	leaf, stem, stalk
SPRING STAGGERWEEDS AND CULTIVATED ORNAMENTALS of *Dicentra* (bleeding-heart), *Corydalis spp*.	top growth, corms
ORNAMENTAL SHRUBS: often potted house, flowering or decorative tropicals; *daphne spp*., boxwood (*Buxus*), *Nerium oleander spp.*, yew (*Taxus*), azalea and other heath family shrubs; privet.	all parts poisonous fruit (berries) are attractive to children and pets of all kinds.
LEGUMES: rosary pea (*Arbrus precatorius*)	all parts but the seed
Black locust (*Robinia*)	bark, green growth, and likely, seeds
Wisteria, horse beans, java beans, loco weeds, and lupines have toxic principles. Crotalaria may be an ornamental.	seeds, especially
SPURGES AND SIMILAR PLANTS: poinsettia, snow-on-the-mountain; castor bean and croton seeds.	all parts, especially seeds
BUTTERCUPS: monkshood (*Aconitum*) foxglove (*digitalis*)	all parts, seed is potent
larkspur (*Delphinium*)	flowers and seeds
peony (*Peony officinalis*)	roots
buttercups (*Ranunculus*) most species	all top growth
NIGHTSHADES: jimsonweed (*Datura spp.*)	all parts, seed very toxic
eggplant, tomato, potato groundcherry	fruit & tubers edible; green growth, sprouts, toxic
nightshades (*Solanum spp.*) of many species	variable, but toxic
tobacco	all parts
PARSLEYS: poison helmock (*Conium Maculatum*) water hemlock (*Cicuta maculata*)	all parts tubers mostly
TOXIC ROOTS: may-apple (*Podophyllum*), poke (*Phytolacca*) mistletoe	roots berries

*Reprinted by permission *Norden News* Norden Laboratories, Lincoln, Nebraska, Vol. 48, No. I, "Beautiful But Deadly," by Arthur A. Case, MS., D.V.M.

time or another nibble on toxic vegetation. The results can vary from vomiting and mild depression to convulsions, coma, and death. If plant poisoning is suspected, the animal should be taken to a veterinarian as quickly as possible, for he will know what poisonous plants are in his area and can treat the dog with one or another of the many antidotes available for specific plants.

Listed on page 175 are some of the more poisonous plants. The list was compiled by Dr. Arthur A. Case of the School of Veterinary Medicine of the University of Missouri, and is reprinted through the courtesy of *Norden News*, a publication of the Norden Laboratories, Lincoln, Nebraska.

POLICE DOGS: dogs of any breed used by police forces all over the world for patroling buildings, trailing and pursuing persons suspected of crimes, scenting contraband drugs, controlling crowds, and tracking missing persons.

POLISH SHEEPDOG: One of the many strong, hardy herding dogs to be found throughout the world, this breed retains the characteristic white or pale cream coat that was described more than three hundred years ago: ". . . sheep dogs should be all white in color so that they may be easily distinguished from the wolf." This particular breed has a heavy outer coat and an even thicker inner one. Dogs range in height from 23 to 27 inches. (Working: 2)

British Police dogs sit at ease while the NCO, presumably, issues orders of the day.

Polish Sheepdog

POMPOM: the rounded tuft of hair, characteristic in poodles, which is left on the end of the tail when the dog is clipped.

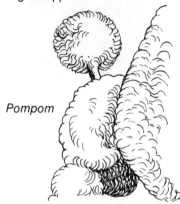
Pompom

POMERANIAN: A member of the Spitz family, this dog sometimes weighed as much as 30 pounds when it first began to draw attention in England not more than a century ago. It gradually was bred down in size and for decades has been a most popular Toy breed. The dog weighs from 3 to 7 pounds in the United States, while 4 to 5½ pounds is standard in Great Britain. Its coat, which in the United States can be virtually any color, solid or parti-colored (in Britain, solid only), is coarse and straight with a soft, thick undercoat. This combination causes the coat to form a profuse frill around the neck. The Pom (Pomerania is in Germany, but no one knows how the dog got its name) is a spirited and intelligent companion, easily trained, but, like most Toys, somewhat wary of rough handling by toddlers. (Toy: 1–2–3–4)

POODLE: Top dog in popularity in the United States since 1969, this dog is a prime favorite in many other countries as well. The Standard Poodle is perhaps the oldest of the three recognized varieties. It was widely used as a retriever of waterfowl (like the Irish Water Spaniel it so closely resembles) and as a circus performer, and some of its ancestors were used to sniff out and uproot truffles. An old breed in very much its present conformation, bas-reliefs of the first century A.D. show representa-

Pomeranian

Standard Poodle

Miniature Poodle

tive specimens. Its coat of thick, springy curls can be any solid color and clipped according to the owner's taste or left untrimmed, in which case the curls turn into cords some four inches long—a choice that has some obvious practical disadvantages. For the show ring, only the Continental or English saddle clips are allowed, though puppies can be shown in the puppy clip. The Standard Poodle must be more than 15 inches tall at the withers and should weigh somewhere between 40 and 55 pounds. (Nonsporting: 1–3–4; Utility: 2)

The Miniature Poodle is the exact replica of the Standard in every way but size—it comes in the same colors and has the same good nature, affectionate disposition, and extraordinarily high intelligence. In England the Miniature must be under 15 inches tall and over 11 inches; in the United States, 15 inches or less, but more than 10. (Nonsporting: 1–3; Utility: 2)

Toy Poodles have the same innate trainability, sturdy health, and nonshedding coats as their bigger brothers and will, what's more, dance if they like the music

Poodles, a versatile breed, can be buffoons or aristocrats, rascals or magical performers.

you are playing, even as the larger varieties do. Size is again the key: in Great Britain Toys are required to be 11 inches tall or less; in the United States, 10 or under. (Toy: 1–3; Utility: 2; Nonsporting: 4)

PORTUGAL: A number of working and sporting breeds originated in Portugal. The local authority is the Clube Portugues de Canicultura, Praca D. Joao Da Camara 4, Lisbon 2.

PORTUGUESE WARREN HOUND: This breed, with its fawn, red, dark-gray, or pied short or long coat, comes in three sizes, depending on what one wants the dog to hunt. For deer, there is the 22 to 27 inch size; for hares, the 20 to 22 inch variety (which can weigh as much as 45 poinds); for rabbits, the small (or pequeno) at 8 to 12 inches in height. Whatever its size or coat, the dog has triangular prick ears and a long tail carried down or in a sickle-like curve. (Hound: 2)

Portuguese Water Dog

teristics. On the seacoast of Portugal this dog is in great demand among fishermen for its ability to retrieve fish that have escaped the net and to recover lines that get separated from the boats. As a natural guard dog it has been useful in protecting the fishermen's boats and possessions. The dog's black-and-white or brown-and-white coat can be either long and somewhat wavy or shorter with flat curls. Height is from 17 to 22½ inches and weight ranges from 35 to 55 pounds. (Working: 2)

Portuguese Warren Hound

PORTUGUESE WATER DOG: This breed has a topknot that looks like a wig added by nature as an afterthought, but its somewhat comical look does not in the least detract from its working charac-

PREFIX: a distinguishing name, often that of a kennel. Thus, the purchasers of dogs from Rainbow Kennel might, for registration purposes, name their dogs *Rainbow's Rusty* or *Rainbow Randy*, etc.

PREGNANCY: the period between breeding (conception) and delivery of the litter (parturition). In a bitch this period usually lasts sixty-three days but may vary from fifty-six to sixty-eight days.

Day 1 to 30: The bitch can continue her normal routine. She will need a well-balanced diet including some extra protein (eggs and

A Great Dane broods maternally over her record-breaking litter of 18 pups.

meat) and calcium in the natural state (skim milk or bone meal). Large quantities of supplements and additives may unbalance an otherwise adequate diet and must be carefully supervised by a veterinarian. The first month is the formative period for the puppies; therefore, worm medicines, dips, and other medications should not be administered to a pregnant bitch unless absolutely necessary, as it is known that many drugs can cause abortion or lead to anomalies of development.

Day 28 to 35: A veterinarian can usually diagnose pregnancy during this week. The owner should now start to collect the equipment needed for delivery. This will include:

l. *Whelping boxes*—cardboard cartons with one side cut down so that the bitch can get in and the pups cannot get out. Three or four are needed so that they may be replaced as they become soiled. If the bitch is one of the larger breeds, cartons from a local market or appliance dealer are free and functional.

2. For more durable quarters, a plywood box can be built with a horizontal half-inch round rail set two inches off the floor and away from the sides all around the inside of the box, so that the bitch cannot crush any pups that get behind her. One side should be removable or cut down to allow the bitch to get in or out.

3. An *overhead heating lamp* may be needed. Young puppies (one to ten days old) are cold-blooded, have no heat-regulating mechanism, and therefore require a temperature of at least 80 degrees.

4. A *heating pad* and *shoe box*, in case it is necessary to remove the pups during delivery.

5. Lots of *newspapers*.

6. Clean, soft *towels*.

Day 45 to 55: The bitch now shows obvious signs of pregnancy. Her abdomen is enlarged and the mammary glands begin to develop. During this period some bitches may become restless and even refuse to eat for a few days.

Day 55 to 63: The bitch should be encouraged to take gentle exercise so that her muscles will remain strong and allow her to whelp easily. During this time she should be carefully watched for early signs of parturition. (See also *whelping*.)

PREMATURE BIRTH (abortion): quite rare in the bitch. It may be caused by an accident, extreme emotional stress, or venereal disease due to *Brucella canis*. Premature puppies born after the fifty-sixth day are often completely developed (except for lack of hair on the nose and feet), and can survive and grow normally to adulthood.

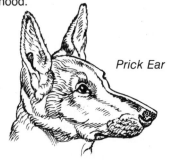

Prick Ear

PRICK EAR: an ear carried straight up and generally pointed at the tip.

PRINCE CHARLES SPANIEL: a tricolor variety of the King Charles Spaniel, which has black-and-tan markings on a pearly white coat, often with a white blaze between the eyes.

Many owners hire professional handlers to show their dogs.

PROFESSIONAL HANDLER: principally in the United States, individuals who are licensed by the American Kennel Club to groom dogs for shows and display their fine points in the ring. They are licensed either to keep dogs in their own boarding kennel and travel with them to shows, or to take over a dog at a show and to groom and put it through its paces during a specific event. Handlers generally specialize in particular breeds or families—Retrievers, for example, or Toys.

Handlers keep all prize money and charge rather high fees, but their skill at grooming and ability to get the best possible results from a dog in the judging ring make them indispensable to many dog owners.

PROTOZOAN DISEASES: a group of diseases caused by one-celled microscopic organisms. Included are coccidiosis, entamoeba giardiasis, balantidiasis, and

181

Much psychological research remains to be done before we attain a more complete understanding of a dog's emotional and intellectul response mechanism.

recognize and greet enthusiastically someone who passed out of his life years before.

Cats, rats, and even parrots are better solvers of "maze" problems than dogs. Whereas these animals study and often solve an imposed dilemma, a dog will only bark. Thus, when a dog barks outside a closed door he is not "asking to be let in." He barks because he is frustrated.

On the other hand the dog gets higher grades than other animals in problems involving spatial relationships. If food is placed behind a screen panel, the dog immediately goes around the screen to get the food, a solution beyond reach of a cat.

These are but a sampling of the tests that have been made in the psychological and psychiatric fields. Those interested in further study are referred to the specialized works cited at the end of this volume.

trichomoniasis, which are infections of the intestinal tract. In the blood stream are found the protozoans *Babesia canis* (one cause of canine tick fever) and *Haemobartonella* (rare in dogs, but common in cats).

PROUD: held high.

PSYCHOLOGY: Since the days of Pavlov and the conditioned reflex, dogs have been the subject of psychological experimentation to determine their intelligence level and reach a better understanding of their emotional responses. Here are a few of the generally accepted results:

While a dog's true memory span is extremely short, his associative memory is remarkable. Thus, a dog (almost certainly because of his remarkable sense of smell) will

PUDELPOINTER: German sportsmen are responsible for having bred this dog—a combination of the fast, reliable Pointer with the latter-day progeny of what used to be called the Hunting Poodle, a shaggy-coated animal with good sense and courage. The result is a fine hunting dog, eligible for registry in the breed stud book only if it has qualified at field trials. The brown coat (which can have sparse white, black-dapple, or fawn markings) is harsh, wiry, and

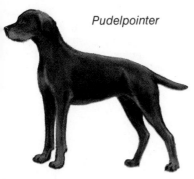

Pudelpointer

companions, being alert, loving, and very adaptable. Their short, sleek coats require a minimum of grooming. Colors may be apricot or silver-fawn or solid black. A black muzzle and mask around the eyes and black ears must accompany the fawn color. Pugs weigh from 14 to 18 pounds and are generally from 10 to 11 inches high. (Toy: 1–2–3–4)

Pug

medium-long, with strong, coarse eyebrows and beard. Dogs stand from 21 to 25½ inches in height. (Sporting: 3)

PUG: Probably a native of China, home of most short-nosed dogs with tightly curled tails, this square, cobby breed came to England with traders representing the Dutch East India Company, became pets of the nobility, and have remained popular ever since. Pugs are good

PULI: An old breed developed in its Hungarian homeland as a driver and herder of sheep, the Puli is a confident, agile worker, known to actually run across the backs

Puli pups look like stuffed animals out of a child's nursery.

Puli

of the sheep in a flock in order to get at a source of trouble. A striking characteristic of the breed is its heavy, weather-resistent coat, black, gray, or white in color. If uncombed, the woolly, dense undercoat tangles with the long, heavy outer coat to form long, tight matted cords. Called the Hungarian Puli (Pulik is the plural) in England, it is frequently brushed and groomed to eliminate the cords if kept as a house pet. This strong, intelligent dog ranges in height from 14 to 19 inches, depending on the country in which it is registered, and weighs about 30 pounds. (Working: 1–3)

PULSE: A dog's heartbeat ranges from 72 to 100 per minute, much like that oı a human. Big dogs have a lower rate than small ones. The best way to take a dog's pulse is to press one's fingers against the inner fleshy side of the hind leg, well above the knee.

PUPPIES, DEATH OF: This can be a source of great disappointment to family breeders and of severe economic loss in larger kennels. There are many causes and often an exact diagnosis cannot be made.

The commonest cause of neonatal death is *chilling*. Young puppies have no heat-regulating mechanism of their own.

Cannibalism is not uncommon, especially in bitches bearing a litter for the first time. Usually due to nervousness, it can be controlled with mild tranquilizers.

Autoimmune or *RH-type reactions* can occur in puppies. The causative factor is secreted in the bitch's milk, and it is often possible to save these pups if they are removed from the breast immediately and nursed by hand.

Hookworm infection, if severe, can cause anemia sufficient to kill a puppy, usually during the fourth to eighth week of life. Other causes of death in puppies include *canine distemper, infectious canine hepatitis,* the recently isolated *herpes virus, bacterial septicemia, brucella infection,* and many others.

PUPPY: any dog under twelve months old.

PYRENEAN MOUNTAIN DOG: see *Great Pyrenees.*

QUARANTINE: the length of time an animal is kept isolated if it is suspected he is the carrier of contagious disease. Rabies is the disease for which quarantine is most commonly used.

QUARANTINE LAWS: differ from country to country. Great Britain demands that dogs and cats being brought into the country be quarantined for six months after having received vaccine in the country from which they embarked. If no symptoms of the disease appear within the time the dog is confined in a special quarantine kennel, he is given a second vaccine and released to his owner.

Australia and New Zealand have much shorter quarantine periods, though they can forbid importation of animals if either country has an outbreak of rabies. The United States does not require dogs or cats being brought into the country to be quarantined.

R

RABIES: a virus disease affecting the nervous system of all warm-blooded animals.

Prevention: Excellent vaccines are now available. They should be given any time after four months of age and repeated as required by local health-department regulations.

Incubation period: one week to one year, but usually three to six months.

Spread: by the bite of an infected animal in the terminal stages of the disease. The incubation period is long because the virus travels slowly along the nerves. However, during this time the animal cannot transmit the disease. When the virus reaches the brain and salivary glands, symptoms appear, the bite becomes infectious, and the animal usually dies within ten days.

RAT TAIL: a tail that is thick at the base and covered with hair but bare at the tip, characteristic of the Irish Water Spaniel.

REGISTRATION: Most kennel clubs around the world maintain stud books or registries in which are entered the names of individual dogs, together with such details as litter date, color, time and place of parents' mating, etc. Since the information required for registration varies widely from country to country—Canada, for example, demands that a registrant be either tattooed or supply a nose-print—one should write to the local canine authorities for instructions.

RESEARCH DOGS: Dogs have contributed greatly to the treatment of many human and canine diseases such as diabetes; modern heart surgery; and the development of antibiotics and other drugs. Contrary to popular belief, these dogs are not usually mistreated. If only for selfish reasons, the scientist must maintain his dogs in good health or his experiments will be meaningless. Dogs are used in research only when cheaper and easier methods (e.g., test tubes, mice) are unlikely to

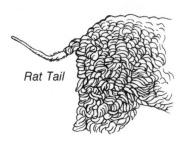

Rat Tail

provide controlled and comparable results. Many scientists now use Beagles that are bred and maintained especially for the purpose. This practice also discourages the unscrupulous dealer who may try to sell a stolen pet to a lab.

Many countries are now evolving laws to regulate the purchase and care of dogs in the laboratory. These laws must be constantly reviewed and adequately enforced to eliminate the illegal dog dealer who is the individual most responsible for cruel treatment of animals.

RESPIRATION: the process by which air is breathed in to supply oxygen to the rest of the body. The normal rate varies greatly, being twenty to twenty-five breaths per minute in a Great Dane and up to sixty-five or more in a Chihuahua. It is usually increased during periods of excitement or stress.

If a dog stops breathing, artificial respiration can sometimes save its life. There are two approved methods. The first, for adult dogs, is executed as follows: place the dog in a prone position, with its sternum, or breastbone, parallel to the ground. With the palms of the hands push gently forward on the rib cage to expel air from the lungs. Release the hands smartly. Repeat this motion every 1½ to 2 seconds for a small dog. Use a bit slower pace for a large one. Because puppies' bones are soft and easily damaged, the following alternate method is generally used: the owner places his mouth over the puppy's muzzle and breathes air into its throat, exercising caution to use only *part* of his air supply. This should be repeated at short intervals until the puppy resumes breathing. Oxygen, if available, should always be used, especially in cardiac patients.

RHEUMATISM: a term loosely used to describe many painful chronic diseases of the joints and muscles. In spite of much research, little is known about many of these conditions. When a dog shows signs of rheumatism (stiffness or pain on moving), the owner should always check with a veterinarian to obtain a positive diagnosis. For home treatment one aspirin per 15 pounds of body weight may be given three to four times daily to reduce the pain temporarily.

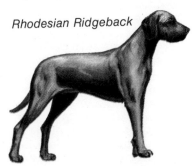

Rhodesian Ridgeback

RHODESIAN RIDGEBACK: A South African native, this large dog (24 to 27 inches tall and weighing from 65 to 75 pounds) evolved as the result of crosses between dogs brought into the country more than three hundred years ago by imigrants and the hunting dog of the native Hottentots. The distinctive "ridge"—a line of hair that grows forward along the back—which was characteristic of the native dog, continues to this day. Good hunters on anything from partridge to lions, these wheaten-colored (light to red) dogs adapt to extreme changes of temperature, have a camel-like ability to go without water for long periods, have sleek, short coats that make them ideal for locales where ticks abound, and are quiet, easily trained when young, and loyal to their human families. (Hound: 1–2–3–4)

RING: arena where dogs are judged.

RING TAIL: a tail carried up and over the back almost in a circle.

RINGWORM (dermatophytosis): a disease of the skin caused by fungi of the genera *Microsporum, Trichophyton,* and others. It occurs in dogs of all breeds and ages, but is usually most severe in animals under one year of age. Ringworm first appears as a round, gray, hairless area that tends to enlarge radically. It is spread by contact— either directly (dog to dog) or indirectly via infected objects, such as fences, lampposts, or kennels. Soil is the source of *Microsporum gypseum.* Several forms of ringworm can spread from dog to man and vice versa. Treatment is available and is usually effective if continued for a sufficient period.

ROACH BACK: a convex curvature (arch) of the back toward the loin.

ROMAN NOSE: high-bridge, slightly hooked.

ROTTWEILER: Named for the township of Rottweil in southern Germany's Württemberg, the ancestors of this dog drove the cattle that fed the Roman legions when they were conquering Central Europe. The Romans helped themselves to Württemberg in the first century and the area, a grain and livestock market center, has been host to this breed ever since. Some specimens were very large and used for pulling carts; smaller animals drove farm animals to market. This medium-large dog (21¾ to 27 inches tall) is such a good guardian that it often carried its master's purse around its neck during a buying trip. Holdup men had no wish to tangle with such fierce, loyal guardians. Perhaps from this aptitude came the sound idea, early in this century, that the dog could be easily trained for police work. The Rottweiler has a short, flat, black coat with distinct body markings that can range from tan to mahogany. (Working: 1–2–3; Nonsporting: 4)

Rottweiler

ROUNDWORM (Ascaridia toxacara): the common puppy worm. The adult worms are one to three inches long and live in the stomach and intestine. Their life cycle is similar to that of the hookworm. Roundworms are not bloodsuck-

Roundworm

Mongrel pets are paraded down London's Oxford Street by anti-vivisectionists, in protest against individuals who give dogs as Christmas presents to children who are not able to care for them properly.

ers but live on the dog's intestinal contents. Due to their large size, they can cause indigestion or even obstruction of the intestine (especially in young puppies). Effective treatments are available, but many of them are potential poisons and the dosage must be carefully calculated. Thus, home treatment by amateurs is not recommended unless done under the supervision of a veterinarian.

ROYAL SOCIETY FOR THE PREVENTION OF CRUELTY TO ANIMALS: The oldest such protection group in the world, the society was formed in 1824 by a London clergyman who resolved to see that a recently passed act of Parliament designed to assure protection of domestic animals would be enforced. The more than two hundred inspectors now employed investigate twenty thousand or so complaints of cruelty to animals yearly. In addition, the society gives free veterinary care at a network of hospitals, clinics, and mobile units in England and Wales; gives first-aid and other advice to pet owners; places animals in new homes; and maintains an air hostel at London Airport, through which more than a million animals pass annually.

RUFF: thick hair around the neck, longer than the rest of the coat.

RUNT: an undersized puppy.

RUPTURE: see *hernia*.

RUSSIAN WOLFHOUND: see *Borzoi*.

S

SABLE: golden, brown, or black hairs laced over a lighter ground color.

SADDLE: a solid color, usually black, marking that looks like a saddle over the back.

SAINT BERNARD: World-famous as a rescuer of lost travelers in the Swiss Alps, this dog of awesome size is now enjoying popularity as a companion and guardian of the home. In its native land the Saint

The Saint Bernard's aptitude for rescue missions led Victorian dog lovers to overestimate its capabilities for this sort of work. It is highly unlikely that this rescue ever took place.

Bernard is still being used to rescue lost or injured skiers and avalanche victims. A truly giant breed, the English standard claims "the taller, the better . . . ." while the American standard calls for a minimum height of 27½ inches for males and 25½ inches for bitches. Two varieties are recognized today: one with a dense, short, smooth coat; the other with medium-long, slightly wavy hair (the result of crosses with the New-foundland in about 1830). Both varieties are white with red, red with white, or brindle with white markings and are not to be of just one color or without white. (Working: 1–2–3; Nonsporting: 4)

Saint Bernard

ST. VITUS' DANCE (chorea): a spasmodic twitching of the muscles of almost any part of the body, sometimes a result of distemper. There is no cure known for the condition, but if a dog's entire body is not affected, a twitch in one area does not necessarily mean it can't live a relatively normal life.

SALUKI: A graceful, beautiful sight hound, the Saluki's ancestry dates back possibly to 7000 B.C. Tomb carvings of Sumeria and

Saluki

Egypt show this tall Greyhound (dogs, 23 to 28 inches), with feathered ears, legs, and tail, almost exactly as it looks today. Coveted by Arab sheiks, the Saluki was bred and trained to work with falcons in hunting gazelle. The present-day standard dictates that the Saluki must give an impression of possessing the speed and endurance necessary to bring down and kill a gazelle. In England the Saluki courses hares and races for the mechanical rabbit at dog tracks. Its soft, silky coat can be black and tan, cream, fawn, golden, grizzle and tan, or tricolor (white, black, and tan), or white. In the United States a smooth variety without feathering is recognized. A devoted companion, the dog is affectionate, dignified, unaggressive, and extremely sensitive. (Hound: 1–2–3–4)

SAMOYED: The most glamorous of the Spitz breeds, the Samoyed has for centuries been a herder and guardian of reindeer for its masters, the Samoyed tribes of northwest Asia and northern Europe. Developed as a dog with great strength and endurance in harness, the breed was used as a sledge dog by Arctic explorers.

Samoyed

An excellent pet, this very showy dog is gentle, devoted, adaptable, and obedient. For show, dogs must be 19 to 23½ inches tall in the United States, 18 to 22 inches in Great Britian. The weather-resistant double coat must be pure white, cream, white and biscuit, or all biscuit. Any other color is considered a disqualification, as are blue eyes. Adding to the charms of the breed are the typical "Samoyed expression"—a very attentive, lively look—and the essential "Samoyed smile"—a slight upward curve of the black lips. (Working: 1–2–3)

SCALING TEETH: Dogs, like man, can build up large quantities of hard tartar at the junction of teeth and gums. If not removed regularly, this tartar can infect the gums and cause the teeth to loosen and fall out. Some experienced owners are able to keep their dogs' teeth clean by frequent use of a dental scraper. This treatment is usually performed by a veterinarian, if necessary, under sedation. Older dogs, especially those with heart or kidney diseases, should have their teeth checked regularly and the tartar removed as needed.

SCENT: The odor left by an animal.

SCENT HURDLE RACING: A new and fast-growing adjunct to obedience training, hurdle racing was developed several years ago in the United States by Herbert O. Wegner. Two teams, each consisting of four dogs and their handlers, compete. One dog from each team races simultaneously over a series of four hurdles spread ten feet apart. Once a dog clears the hurdles he must detect the scent of his handler on one of a number of wooden dumbbells placed on a raised platform positioned twelve feet beyond the last hurdle and return that particular dumbbell

The Belgian Sheepdog has a slight edge over the Norwich Terrier as the dogs start over the hurdles.

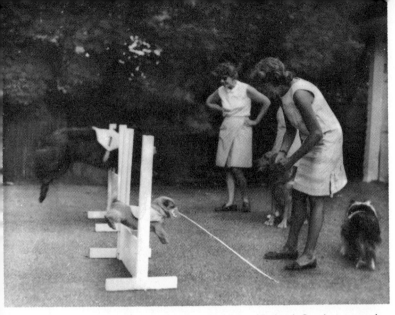

(Above) The tiny Norwich wins by a whisker. (Below) So that crowds can view hurdle racing from a distance, colors are used on dog vests, platforms, and dumbbells.

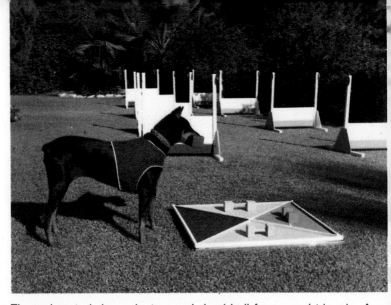

The red-vested dog selects a red dumbbell from a red triangle. Any other color choice would spell total failure.

over the hurdles to his handler before the next dog on the team is sent to repeat the same performance. As soon as a dumbbell is removed, another is put in its place, so each dog must make the proper selection from four possibilities. After each heat the platform is rotated a quarter turn so that the dumbbells are always in a different position. The first team to win two out of three heats is declared victor.

SCHIPPERKE: This dog gets its name from the Flemish word for "little captain," since in the

Schipperke

nineteenth century it was often used as a guard on canal boats. As a breed, this tailless (born so or docked), energetic little dog has a history that goes back several hundred years. Though an eager hunter of rabbits and small vermin, the Schipperke, with its happy personality, intense curiosity, and gentle ways with children, is generally regarded as an excellent family companion and guardian of the home. It is a small (up to 18 pounds in the United States, 12 to 16 pounds in Britian), cobby dog, with a foxy head, small erect ears, and a bright expression that gives it a mischievous look. Its short, dense, black coat forms a heavy ruff and cape around the neck and shoulders and a culotte on the back side of the thighs. In the United States any color other than a solid jet black is a disqualification, as are button or semi-erect ears. In England a coat of any solid color is

194

permissible. (Nonsporting: 1–3–4; Utility: 2)

SCHNAUZER: The word means "snout," and each of the three types of dogs is judged in a class by itself. (See also *Giant Schnauzer, Miniature Schnauzer,* and *Standard Schnauzer*.)

SCHUTZHUND: Translated from the German, it means "protection dog." Currently, thirty-seven nations are training Schutzhunds and all are working under the rules of the World Dog Federation, or FCI (Fédération Cynologique Internationale), with headquarters in Belgium. The term "Schutzhund" applies principally to the German Shepherd, but also includes the Doberman, Rottweiler, Giant Schnauzer, Boxer, Airedale, and several other FCI-recognized working breeds.

This widely accepted technique of working-dog training consists of three parts: tracking, obedience, and protection work. A dog has to show good temperament and physical fitness to qualify for training. Degrees, as internationally recognized, are Schutzhund 1 (Sch. 1), Schutzhund 2 (Sch. 2), and Schutzhund 3 (Sch. 3). A dog must attain a minimum score in all three categories to receive a degree. With Schutzhund 2 and 3, the exercises become progressively more demanding.

After Schutzhund training a dog can move on to advanced tracking (FH), endurance tests, police-dog examinations (PD), and others.

Schutzhund training is a sport that requires hard work and should only be undertaken by persons dedicated to the ideal of the "Total Dog."

In Schutzhound training the handler searches a suspect for weapons. The dog is alert, ready to attack should the suspect attempt to flee.

SCISSORS BITE: a bite in which the outer side of the lower incisor teeth touches the inner side of the upper incisors.

SCOTCH COLLIE: see *Collie*.

Scottish Deerhound

SCOTTISH DEERHOUND: These thick-coated aristocrats, the largest members of the Greyhound family, were clan favorites in the Highlands for many centuries. Today, with deerstalking a sport of the past, they are less frequently seen. These amiable and affectionate giants range up to 110 pounds in weight and more than 30 inches at the withers in America; a bit less in the U.K. (Hound: 1–2–3–4)

SCOTTISH TERRIER: One of five breeds of Terrier that originated in Scotland, all of which were used by farmers and sportsmen to "go to ground" after the fox, the Scottie

Scottish Terrier

has been bred in its present purity for close to a hundred years. It is a small, sturdily built dog (10 inches tall and weighing 18 to 22 pounds—a shade bigger in England) with a distinctive beard, small, erect ears, a slightly curved tail carried straight up in the air, and a harsh, wiry coat of medium length. Allowable colors are jet black (seen most frequently), steel gray, brindled or grizzled, sand or wheaten. A perfect dog for apartment dwellers, this extremely independent, spunky Terrier makes an interesting companion and a tough little watchdog. (Terrier: 1–2–3–4)

SEALYHAM TERRIER: Though little is positively known about this substantial, short-legged sporting Terrier's ancestry, it is known that its development was started in the 1850's by Captain John Edwardes at his estate, Sealyham, in Pembrokeshire, Wales. Plucky, fearless fighters were selected to produce a strain of Terrier that would be small in size and possess sufficient strength and endurance to dig out passageways and go underground in pursuit of badgers or other quarry.

This handsome Terrier, with a bushy beard, ears folded level with the top of its head, and a typical, weather-resisting wiry top coat with a dense, soft undercoat, is white in color, sometimes with lemon, badger, or tan head and ear markings. The United States breed standard calls for a height of 10½ inches at the withers and a weight of 20 to 21 pounds, with the reminder that in this breed, size is a more important consideration than weight. In England a maximum of 12 inches in height and

Sealyham Terrier

20 pounds in weight is specified. An even-tempered, lighthearted dog, despite its aggressive ancestors, the Sealyham is an intelligent, companionable family pet. (Terrier: 1–2–3–4)

SHEDDING: a normal function of the skin when old hairs become loose, fall out, and are replaced by new ones. The process is to some extent continuous (especially in house pets), but is greatest during the period when the dog is undergoing a seasonal change of coat.

Shedding occurs in all breeds, but is said to be less in some —Poodles and Kerry Blue Terriers, for example. Regular grooming removes the dead hair from the coat, and by stimulating circulation, helps encourage new hair growth.

Excessive shedding can be caused by a variety of conditions, such as dry heat in the home, lack of essential fatty acids in the diet, internal parasites, and hormonal or other biochemical imbalances. Veterinary diagnosis and treatment should be sought.

SEX PLAY: There is no known way to prevent dogs, from puppyhood onward, from mounting one another, regardless of sex or age. While such behavior may momentarily distress an owner or guests with delicate sensibilities, it is harmless and will generally be of short duration.

More serious is the habit of some dogs of attaching themselves to visitors' or childrens' legs or objects in the home or street. A sharp command, accompanied by a vigorous jerk on the dog's collar to detach him from the momentary object of his affection, may possibly break him of the habit if repeated often enough, but this is by no means certain.

If a dog's misguided sex urge leads him into a continued pattern of offensive behavior, the owner might consider castration. It is a radical cure but one that is almost sure to have the desired result.

SHEEPDOG TRAINING: Sheepdogs herd chiefly by instinct. Training is mostly a matter of refining those instincts and begins with standard obedience training when the puppy is old enough to obey commands. The potential herding dog is not trained to heel, however, for it has to learn to work away from its master. Before puppies are allowed to run sheep, which they instinctively try to do at somewhere between six and ten months of age, they must learn to drop on command. The youngsters have to be old enough to possess the strength and speed needed to run *around* the sheep, for they must not chase them from behind or nip at the first of the flock they reach. Thus, the importance of the "drop," which prevents the formation of bad habits in early training. This is serious work and not a game. Young dogs are allowed to watch experienced sheepdogs work, but are not permitted to run with them.

A guardian warily eyes its charges in a British Sheepdog Trial.

SHEEPDOG TRIALS: held in Australia, England, New Zealand, Scotland, the United States, and Wales, as well as elsewhere in the world, though the first trial was a Welsh event held in 1873. Dogs work under natural conditions rounding up sheep, driving them, and bringing them in groups to sheds, pens, or a ring. Border Collies bred for trials are the chief performers in England. Registration in the studbook of Britain's International Sheepdog Society is extremely selective. In order for a dog to be registered in the North American Sheepdog Society, it has to be certified as coming from working parentage.

SHETLAND   SHEEPDOG: Though this breed resembles the Rough Collie in miniature, it is thought that the Shetland Sheepdog was not bred down to its diminutive size from the Collie, but rather that both breeds share a common

Shetland Sheepdog

ancestor—perhaps the Border Collie. An agile, swift, and clever working dog, the Sheltie was adept at managing flocks of the small Shetland Island sheep. Though capable of handling the larger breeds of sheep outside its native homeland, the Shetland Sheepdog now enjoys tremendous popularity as a family companion and as a fast, accurate worker in obedience competition.

The dog's heavy Collie-like coat, with profuse mane and frill, may be sable, black, or blue merle with white and/or tan markings. Height at the shoulders ranges from 13 to 16 inches with dogs measuring above or below those limits being disqualified in United States show rings.(Working:1–2–3–4)

Shih Tzu

SHIH TZU: These royal dogs of China have been around for a long time, although exactly when they arrived at court is not known. In the mid-seventeenth century responsibility for breeding the Shih Tzu was delegated to eunuchs in the Emperor's court who competed to produce specimens of "the chrysanthemum-faced dog" sufficiently superior to engage the imperial fancy and thus win prizes for themselves. The dogs look not only like chrysanthemums, but like miniature lions, and it is from this that their name comes. These short-faced dogs with their long, dense, somewhat wavy coats, hair falling over the eyes, long, heavily-coated ears, and thickly plumed tails, are merry, tractable pets in the Western world, though in their homeland they often do indoor guard duty. Any coat color is permissible for the breed, which should be from 8 to 11 inches tall and weigh from 9 to 18 pounds. (Toy: 1)

SHOCK: a complex condition in which the blood pressure falls so that the tissues of the body are unable to get sufficient oxygen for normal functioning. It is usually caused by a serious injury or overwhelming infection. Shock is always an emergency and requires immediate intensive veterinary treatment. However, the owner can often save the dog's life by keeping it warm with blankets until professional help is obtained.

Signs of shock include coldness of the body, a rapid, weak pulse, and paleness of the mucous membranes. An owner can recognize shock by a simple test. Press a finger firmly on the dog's gum for one to two seconds so that the area blanches. Normally, this white area will disappear instantly, but during shock it may persist for five seconds or longer.

SHOWS: The Kennel Club, founded in 1873, is the governing body for dog shows in England. It registers more than 150 different breeds that are divided into two main divisions—Sporting Dogs and Nonsporting. Each of these is

199

Standing dogs for examination more than twenty years ago at Westminster. Techniques of judging have changed little over the years.

further broken down into three groups. Sporting encompasses Hounds, Gundogs, and Terriers; Nonsporting includes Utility, Working, and Toy dogs. There are up to twenty classes at shows on a graded scale, based on wins at previous shows, and the shows are either open to all exhibitors, or to members only. There are hundreds of events annually, ranging from informal matches to championship affairs. Prize money is low, and as a matter of policy entry fees are similarly small.

In the United States the American Kennel Club governs the running of most dog shows, of which there are more than a thousand. These are either all-breed or specialty or single-breed championship events. As befits the most populous state, California has the largest number of shows, but there are events everywhere from Rhode Island to Hawaii. The United States registers fewer breeds than Great Britain—some 120—and divides all prospective show entrants into six groups: Sporting, Hounds, Working, Terriers, Toys, and Nonsporting. Some of the bigger shows, like the Westminster, have had to limit entries for lack of space for benching; others have given up benching entirely. Many shows are part of a circuit in which a number of events are held in an approximate two-week span. The AKC also conducts close to a thousand field trials for individual breeds as well as an increasing number of obedience trials. *American Field—Field Dog Stud Book* also conducts field trials, chiefly for English Setters and Pointers. Specific information about shows held under its auspicies can be obtained from the AKC.

In Canada the Canadian Kennel Club, which registers more than

130 breeds, supervises a variety of championship shows, but, obviously, fewer in number than in the States. There is no licensing of professional handlers in Canada, and all dogs eligible must remain for group judging. Otherwise, ring regulations are much like those in the United States. Dogs are divided for show-entry purposes into the following six groups: Sporting Dogs, Sporting Dogs (Hounds), Working Dogs, Terriers, Toys, and Nonsporting Dogs. As with other national kennel clubs, the Canadian Kennel Club will provide information on request about the rules and regulations governing the shows in that country.

SHYNESS: A dog is said to be shy when it overreacts to normal, non-threatening situations. Shyness can be inherited, but more often it is due to some frightening experience during the period of character development (two to ten weeks of age) or to a general lack of socialization. Shyness can usually be greatly reduced by gentle treatment and training, but is likely to recur during periods of stress throughout the dog's life. In its extreme form it can result in fear biting. Without any apparent provocation, a dog so afflicted may bite its master or any other member of the family. If this happens more than once, consult your veterinarian promptly, whether or not the bites have been severe.

SIBERIAN HUSKY: The Chukchi, a semi-nomadic tribe of northeastern Siberia, was responsible for developing this animal, which could pull a loaded sled for miles

Siberian Husky

in the coldest imaginable weather without tiring. Word of its prowess spread to Alaska early in this century, and teams of Huskies, in relays, were used in the world-famous run to carry diphtheria antitoxin to the stricken city of Nome in 1925. They were with Commander Byrd at the Antarctic, and served in the Arctic during World War II as part of the Search and Rescue Unit.

The Siberian Husky is a strikingly handsome dog with a dense, straight coat of medium length that

Siberian Huskies make fine pets as well as good work dogs.

201

can be of any color. Head markings, many of which are seen in no other breed, are varied, with a pattern that resembles a cap and a pair of spectacles perhaps the most common. Eye color varies, too, for in addition to the usual brown color, China-blue eyes are permitted. One or both eyes may be blue or blue mixed with brown (parti-colored). A medium-sized dog (height, 20 to 23½ inches; weight, 35 to 60 pounds) the Siberian is a friendly, outgoing breed, and especially fond of children. It is not by nature a possessive guard dog, nor is it usually aggressive with other dogs.

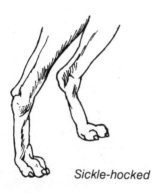

Sickle-hocked

SICKLE-HOCKED: having stifles well bent and hocks very low with an exaggerated bend; characteristic of fast runners like the Greyhound.

SICKLE TAIL: A tail carried up and out in a half circle.

SIGHT: It is believed that dogs see less well than humans by day, better at night. They are colorblind, or nearly so, and particularly bad at spotting stationary objects a considerable distance from them.

When an object begins to move, however, the dog spots it instantly. Thus, a sight Hound will follow every motion of its prey in the pursuit. It is possible, however, that a dog's sense of smell and hearing supplement its vision at times like this.

Studies made in recent years indicate that a dog's eyes see shapes fuzzily and do not distinguish details. Myopia is common, particularly in Bulldogs, Pugs, and other breeds with protruding eyes.

The field vision varies considerably from breed to breed. Many Sheepdogs, for example, have poor frontal vision but excellent peripheral vision, which enables them to spot wanderers from the herd out of the corner of one eye.

At night a substance called "visual purple" begins to function in a dog, expanding the pupils and allowing more light to enter. Rhodopsin, as it is technically called, is vitamin A and protein, and if it is not present, night blindness occurs, in humans as well as dogs.

Point a flashlight at a dog in the night and you will note that its

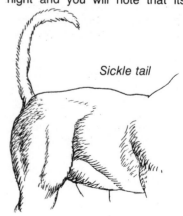

Sickle tail

eyes shine with color—a reflection of the shiny part of the retina which is visible through the enlarged pupil.

Silky Terrier

SILKY TERRIER: This small, light, and lively dog originated in Sydney, Australia, as a result of a cross between the Yorkshire Terrier and the Australian Terrier. Though not known outside Australia until after 1909, it has gained steadily in popularity as an enchanting family pet.

A low-set dog, the Silky Terrier stands 9 to 10 inches at the shoulder and weighs 8 to 10 pounds. Its silky, rich blue and tan, long coat, 5 to 6 inches in length for the body coat, is parted down the midline from nose to tail. A topknot is formed by long, thick hair on the forehead, silver or fawn in color. Though classified as a Toy breed, the Terrier characteristics and keen spirit of the breed are highly valued. Exaggerated toyishness detracts from the desired Terrier image and is faulted in the show ring. (Toy: 1–2–3–4)

SKYE TERRIER: One of the oldest of the Terrier breeds, the Skye seen in today's show ring is a larger dog with a coat even more exaggerated in length than that of the Skye Terrier that some four hundred years ago went to ground after badger or fox in its native land, the Isle of Skye. A favorite at court during the reign of Elizabeth I, the breed continued to be popular with British royalty, and by the end of the nineteenth century it was considered the most popular of all Terriers.

It is a low, long-bodied dog, its length being twice its height (10 inches at the shoulder), with a long, heavily feathered tail. Gracefully fringed ears may be either medium-sized, erect and set rather high on the head, or larger button ears set slightly lower and folded flat against the head. The tremendous coat, with a desired length of 5½ inches, is parted down the length of the body from head to tail and falls profusely over the forehead, protecting the eyes of the working Terrier from injury. Coat color may be a light to dark gray, blue, black, silver, fawn, or cream with the points of the muzzle, the ears, and the tip of the tail being black.

A reserved dog with strangers, the Skye is a devoted and entertaining pet at home and serves as a competent watchdog. (Terrier: 1–2–3–4)

Skye Terrier

SLED DOG: While dogs have been used for centuries to pull carts (generally for the milkman or florist) it is in the frozen Arctic that the dog comes into its own as a draught animal. There are many types of pure-bred sled dogs, not only the AKC recognized Siberian Husky, Samoyed and Alaskan Malamute, but the Eskimo dog and Greenland, Mackenzie River and Indian Huskies as well. Greenland and Mackenzie River Huskies weigh about 100 pounds, the Indian Husky about half as much.

Sled dogs work in teams, hauling big loads over vast distances, in temperatures that drop to minus 40 degrees Fahrenheit, in blizzards with winds that mount to 100 m.p.h. They see little of their human masters, remaining in harness throughout the frozen nights curled up in the snow. The lead

dog in a pack is harnessed by itself and, in a sense, is manager of the pack. The lead dog, whether utilized for pack or racing, is chosen for its speed, drive, enthusiasm and endurance. In earlier times (the Siberian Husky has been domesticated for at least 30 centuries) the Steppe tribesmen drove their packs with whips and goads, but today lead dogs and packs undergo training not unlike that employed in obedience rings.

The myth that Husky-type dogs are vicious is completely without foundation. The harsh treatment they received over the centuries naturally caused many dogs to turn on humans, but a well-treated Husky is as amiable as any of his canine relatives.

The unrecognized Alaskan and/or Indian Husky and the Siberian Husky are used most frequently in racing; Malamutes, Samoyeds and Eskimos are employed in freighting and seldom race.

SLED-DOG RACES: held in northern lands all over the world when there is enough snow to support a sled, a driver, and a team, consisting of from one to fifteen dogs. Canine competitors are most often Alaskan and/or Indian Huskies and Siberians. The world championship takes place yearly in Anchorage, Alaska, where teams must run a twenty-five mile course daily on three successive days. Any number of dogs can compete on a given team, but to qualify, every dog on the team has to be present at the finish, even

While actual sleds used in racing are made of ash and weigh less than 40 pounds, far heavier wheel-gigs, like this one, are used in training dogs for the sport. As many as sixteen dogs may pull the gig in a training session

A racing team in good form—all in step and running at top speed. Most top teams run at about 17 mph average for about 20 miles.

The Quebec Husky, a special breed used in sled racing, was developed some forty years ago by crossing Siberian Huskies with German Shepherds and Greyhounds.

if it has to be carried across the line on the sled driver's shoulders. Racing sleds used in present-day competition are light snow skimmers, not pack sleds.

Sled dog racing began in North America in 1908 and the sport is today governed by the International Sled Dog Racing Association (ISDRA). Aptitude, speed, drive and endurance are the four qualities breeders of racing dogs look for.

The snowmobile has replaced dogteams for U.S. postal service in Alaska. Shown here with Harris Dunlap, a top breeder and trainer of sled dogs, are the famous Siberian Racing Husky, Wawa, and Anna, an Alaskan, or Indian, Husky.

SLEEP AND DREAMS: As in humans, sleep in animals is a cyclical affair, ranging from semiwakefulness to deep sleep and to the so-called oneiric period when dreams take place. During its dreams a dog's lips will tremble or extend into a smile or a snarl; the extremities will twitch; it will groan or whimper or make little whining noises. Gundogs will make movements that clearly are associated with the chase. More precise interpretations of dog dreams are lacking, however, and await the appearance of a latter-day Freud.

SMELL: It is often said that a dog's sense of smell is its mind, since in this one sensory area the canine aptitude is amazing. If a dog cannot see something it is looking for, it "stares," but this puzzled attitude rarely if ever occurs when the animal's nose is concerned. An average dog can detect one drop of blood in five quarts of water; it can smell a bone burried more than two feet underground or a bird or animal more than two hundred feet away. Once the dog picks up the scent, it will lose the trail only if the animal, human or otherwise, crosses a river or gets into a moving vehicle, with its feet not touching the ground. Where a fresh track is concerned —and "fresh" may mean up to eight hours old—a dog's nose never betrays it. A French scientist adds that the moist nose of a healthy dog plays its role in this phenomenon: "it is this wet surface that retains, and in some fashion absorbs, the emanations floating in the air." Wet nose or dry, however, a dog has from thirty to fifty times as many olfactory cells in its body as a man does, and they function better, cell for cell, than those in a human.

SNAKEBITE: Veterinarians are rarely close by when a dog is bitten by a venomous snake, so the owner must follow the same first-aid procedures he would employ if he were the victim: (1) apply a tourniquet above the wound; (2) with a knife or razor blade make an incision one-quarter of an inch deep over each fang mark, in the shape of the letter x; (3) suck or press the wound to expel as much of the venom as possible; (4) get the dog to a veterinarian or hospital as quickly as possible. Note: swelling and extreme pain follow a poisonous snakebite. If these symptoms do not occur, or if you are not certain that the snake was poisonous, do nothing. Many dogs bitten by nonpoisonous snakes have been badly cut by overzealous owners.

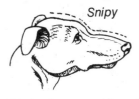
Snipy

SNIPY: having a weak, pointed muzzle.

SOFT-COATED WHEATEN TERRIER: Though a newcomer to the AKC studbook and not even a registered breed in his homeland of Ireland until 1937, this hardy, lively working Terrier is an old breed and has long served as a ratter, stable guardian, and cattle dog.

A distinctive feature of the

Soft-coated Wheaten Terrier

Wheaten is its profuse, moderately long coat that lacks the harsh, wiry texture typical of the outer coat of most other Terriers. The coat is soft, slightly wavy, and is never clipped nor plucked, though it may be tidied up a bit for show purposes. The color may be any shade of ripe wheat from a pale gold to a silvery color, and in immature dogs may vary considerably as the shades progress from the deep red color usual at birth to the final pale wheaten color of the adult.

In the United States the breed standard calls for a height of 18 to 19 inches at the shoulder, with a weight of 35 to 40 pounds for males. Bitches may be somewhat smaller. In Great Britain 17½ inches is the ideal height, and weight can be from 35 to 45 pounds. (Terrier: 1–2)

SOFT MOUTH: a term applied to retrievers that bring back game without chewing or lacerating it.

SOUNDNESS: top mental and physical condition.

SOUTH AFRICA: The Kennel Union of South Africa, P.O. Box 562, Cape Town, closely parallels the regulations of the Kennel Club of England.

SPAIN: For information, write to Real Sociedad Central de las Razas Caninas en Espana, Los Madrazos 20, Madrid, 14.

SPAYING: a procedure in which a bitch's uterus and ovaries are surgically removed via an abdominal incision. The operation can be performed at any age, but is usually recommended before or after the first heat. After spaying, a bitch will not come into season, but will live a normal life in all other respects. Contrary to popular belief, a spayed bitch will not get fat; she may require less food each day, but the operation in no way causes added girth.

SPEED: Greyhounds have been reliably clocked at 37 m.p.h. and a bit more at distances of less than one-half mile. Claims for greater speeds have been made for other breeds, but authentication of this is lacking.

Soft Mouth

SPLASHED: having irregular patches of color on white, or white on color.

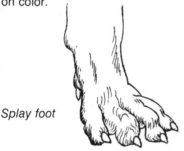

Splay foot

SPLAYFOOT: a flat foot, having spreading toes.

SPITZ BREEDS: No other family of dogs has the variety of breeds, ranging from the tiny Pomeranian to the sturdy Akita, as the Spitz clan. All share in common prick-ears, wedge-shaped heads, dense undercoats to protect them from the biting cold along with straight, usually longish outer coats. Virtually all carry their tails over the back.

Some of the other Spitz dogs are: Samoyed, Keeshond, Eskimo, Norwegian Buhund, Alaskan Malamute, Siberian Husky, Iceland Dog, Norwegian Elkhound, Schipperke, Chow Chow, and Japanese Spitz.

A wedge-shaped head—common to all members of the Spitz family.

SPREAD: the width between the forelegs when it is a point of emphasis, as in the Bulldog.

Staffordshire Bull Terrier

STAFFORDSHIRE BULL TERRIER: Bred originally to fight another dog on a one-to-one basis in a pit with wooden sides, this dog needed the strength and stick-to-itiveness of the Bulldog combined with the Terrier's ability to think and move fast.

Today's typical specimen is medium-sized (14 to 16 inches high and weighing 28 to 38 pounds) with a short, smooth coat that may be white, brindle, or any solid color with the exception of liver or black and tan, and with or without white markings. It has rose or half-pricked ears. Full button ears are faulted in the show ring. The standard specifies that the ears may not be cropped, nor is trimming or removal of whiskers permitted. A muscular dog, giving an impression of great strength for its size, the Staffordshire Bull Terrier is recognized as a reliable, courageous guard dog and as a sensible, and tractable family companion who adapts with equal ease to country or city life. (M: 1; Terrier: 2–3–4).

Staffordshire Terrier

STAFFORDSHIRE TERRIER: Here is a dog that through no fault of its own compounds confusion. First registered in the AKC studbook as the Staffordshire Terrier, its name was changed in 1972 to American Staffordshire Terrier, and in England it is not recognized at all. In the United States these dogs have been variously known as Pit Dogs, Pit Bull Terriers, American Bull Terriers, and Yankee Terriers. Whatever they were called, they were bred for fighting. Often confused with the Staffordshire Bull Terrier, they are nonetheless very different dogs —bigger (17 to 19 inches tall), and heavier, and with half rose or prick ears, which in this breed may be cropped. Their short, stiff coats, though commonly brindle, may be any color. All white or more than 80 per cent white, as well as black and tan or liver, are not favored in the show ring. Today the Staffordshire Terrier is bred to be a gentle dog that is a discerning guard dog as well as a loyal pet. (Terrier: 1–3)

STANDARD SCHNAUZER: This bearded breed, from which the other two Schnauzer breeds were developed, probably originated in the farmlands of southern Germany where it was used as a cattle drover, guard dog, and ratter. To test the breed's capabilities as a ratter, Schnauzer clubs in Germany still sponsor ratting trials.

The medium-sized Schnauzer (18½ to 19½ inches for males, 17½ to 18½ inches for bitches) is a heavy-set, squarely built, muscular dog, with the typical harsh coat of salt and pepper or pure black and the characteristic Schnauzer beard and eyebrows. The Standard Schnauzer combines power, endurance, and agility with intelligence and an eagerness to please that makes him a useful working dog and an extremely satisfying house pet. (Working: 1–3; Utility: 2; Nonsporting: 4)

Standard Schnauzer

STANDOFF COAT: a heavy or long coat that stands away from the body.

STIFLE: Equivalent to the human knee, it is the joint below the femur, or thigh bone, and the tibia. It includes the knee cap or patella.

STILTED: having the choppy gait characteristic of dogs lacking sufficient angulation in front or hind quarters.

STOP: the indentation between the eyes where the nasal bone and skull meet.

Straight-hocked

STRAIGHT-HOCKED: having hock joints that are almost vertical and without angles.

Straight-shoulders

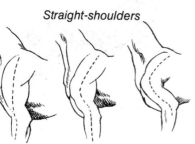

STRAIGHT-SHOULDERS: when shoulder blades are virtually straight up and down instead of sloping, causing the dog to appear very short in neck. The forward reach of a dog with straight shoulders is very restricted, often resulting in a stilted gait.

STUDBOOK: a record of breeding specifics of dogs recognized by kennel clubs.

STUD DOG: a male dog kept for breeding. He should be a superior specimen of his breed and at least one year of age. When mated for the first time, a young stud should be bred to an experienced older bitch. Most stud dogs can be bred at regular intervals and can continue to breed until they are ten or more years of age. Some countries require a veterinarian to observe the mating before they will register the litter sired by a stud over ten years old.

SUICIDE: Despite stories to the contrary, a dog, having no way of appreciating an abstract concept (i.e., death), cannot deliberately end its own life. It is true that if a beloved owner, upon whom a dog depends, suddenly goes out of its existence, the animal may refuse to eat and, theoretically at least, could starve to death. But in virtually all such cases, if the animal is placed in new surroundings and treated with understanding, it will quickly adapt and slip easily into a new routine.

SUSSEX SPANIEL: A comparatively low-slung, heavy-set dog (15 to 16 inches tall and weighing from 35 to 45 pounds), the Sussex Spaniel was accompanying hunters on foot in Sussex at the close of the eighteenth century. It is a determined worker, suited to seeking out upland game in heavy cover; but it lacks the speed and style required by American hunters, and its inclination to give voice while on a scent is a serious fault in trial work. Where conditions require a powerful, careful worker, however, hunters find the Sussex to be a steady and useful companion with a good nose.

Its abundant, flat coat must be a rich golden liver color, darker col-

Sussex Spaniel

SWISS LAUFHUND: Also known as the Jura in England, this dog is a stronger and more heavily built hound than some of the other Swiss breeds (such as the Lucernese and the Schweizer). All date back nearly two thousand years. The Jura is a keen hunter with a good nose and voice. It is distinguished by a heavy domed head, a wrinkled forehead, and large and very long ears. Its short coat can be fawn or tan (black saddle is allowed), or black and tan. Dogs range from 16 to 18 inches tall and are hunting hounds, not indoor dogs. (Hound: 2)

ors indicating a recent cross with the Field Spaniel. Ears are long and well covered with soft, wavy hair. The heavily feathered tail is docked to a length of 5 to 7 inches, and its merry action, typical of most Spaniels, indicates the cheerful disposition of the breed. (Sporting: 1–3; Gundog: 2–4)

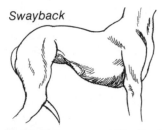

Swayback

Swiss Laufhund

SWAYBACK: a curve of the back, which is concave between withers and hipbones.

SWEDEN: Svenska Kennelklubben, Box 1121, S 11181, Stockholm, is the regulatory canine authority in this country.

SWITZERLAND: Rescue and other working breeds are featured at Swiss shows. The authority is Société Cynologique Suisse, Case Postale 2307. Ch-3001. Berne 1 Facher.

T

TAHLTAN BEAR DOG: A real specialist, this long-coated dog is almost a one-tribe animal—the property of the North American Tahltan tribe. Dogs are kept in a skin pouch until hunters get near their quarry—bear, lynx, or porcupines—and then are released to keep the game at bay until the hunters can get in close to shoot. The dogs are not adaptable to other conditions. They cannot be raised in more clement climates, cannot be persuaded to eat more than miniscule protein snacks at any one time, and cannot be dissuaded from howling like coyotes. These dogs are small (12 to 15 inches high), look much like a fox, and have coats that are all black, blue-gray with patchy white markings, or white with black patches. (Sporting: 3)

Tahltan Bear Dog

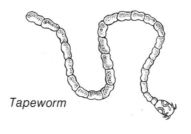

Tapeworm

TAPEWORMS: a long, segmented worm that lives in the intestinal tract. Two species of tapeworms are common in the dog and both have a complicated life history. They must pass through an intermediate host (different species of animals) before returning to the dog to complete their development. Dogs become infected when they eat an intermediate host—by way of example, rabbits (the intermediate host of the Taenia) or the common dog flea (the intermediate host of the Dipylidium). Tapeworms can be recognized in the dog as white or brownish rice-sized segments around the anus and underside of the tail. Treatment is safe, simple, and effective.

TARTAR: see *scaling teeth*.

TATTOOING: Since identification tags can be lost or removed, tattooing is rapidly growing in favor

213

as a means of preventing theft of a family pet or recovering a lost animal. A permanent tattoo, usually on the upper part of the inner right thigh (in the United States the owner's social security number is favored) is painless and takes but a few minutes. It can be performed by a veterinarian or under the auspices of local kennel clubs or animal welfare agencies. The number is then filed with a central agency, and if worn on a tag, can act as a warning to dognappers. Also, research laboratories will not accept a tattooed dog for experimentation, and if one is offered them, can notify local police promptly.

In Canada tattooing as well as a dog's nose prints are part of the registration procedure.

TEAM: ordinarily, four dogs of the same breed being shown together.

TEATS: present in both males and females. Most canines carry five teats on each side of the abdomen, but the number may vary from four to six. During lactation the teats in the bitch are active and greatly enlarged. They should be inspected daily to ensure that they do not become blocked with milk or injured by the nursing puppies.

TEETH: Dogs have two sets of teeth—deciduous (puppy, or temporary) and permanent teeth. There are twenty-eight deciduous teeth, consisting of three incisors, one canine, and three premolars on each side of the upper and lower jaws. Eruption starts at three weeks and is completed by eight weeks.

The dog normally has forty-two permanent teeth, but this number is frequently reduced in the short-nosed breeds. There are three incisors, one canine, four premolars, and two molars on each side of the upper jaw. The lower jaw carries one extra molar tooth (three in all) plus three incisors, one canine and four premolars on each side.

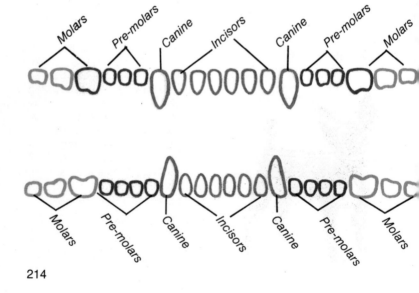

The puppy teeth begin to fall out at four months and are rapidly replaced by the permanent teeth. The permanent canines (fangs) should be fully erupted by six months. If the temporary teeth are still present at this time, a veterinarian should decide whether extraction is needed.

A dog's teeth should be inspected at least once a year and tartar removed regularly as needed. Caries of the teeth is rare in dogs, but pyorrhea and other diseases of the gums are commonly seen and must be treated promptly.

TERRITORIAL RIGHTS: Apparently it is instinct that causes a dog to guard the territory it considers its own against all comers. This instinct is refined in some breeds that have been bred and trained for generations as guardians, though all breeds show some evidence of it. They respect the territory of others, as they expect others to respect theirs. The instinct is often exaggerated beyond reasonable limits in dogs who, as puppies, have been taken away from their litter mates too soon and thus denied socialization at a crucial time.

THIGH: the hindquarter from the hip to the stifle.

THROATINESS: the condition of having more skin than necessary under the throat.

TIBETAN MASTIFF: Nobody knows precisely what this dog's ancestors were, though everybody from Aristotle to Marco Polo has taken a turn at describing the mammoth dog, which was once a big-game hunter as well as a guard

Tibetan Mastiff

for Tibetan herdsmen. These dogs have a long, black, black and tan, or golden coat, a massive head, and a tail as full as a squirrel's, which is generally carried over their backs. They are extremely strong, and it is doubtless from this native characteristic that legends about their prowess have grown up. Representative specimens are from 22 to 27½ inches tall; males weigh about 165 pounds. (Working: 2)

Tibetan Mastiffs are popular in Nepal, but rarely seen elsewhere.

Tibetan Spaniel

TIBETAN SPANIEL: Not a Spaniel at all, as far as anyone knows, the origins of this Pekingese-like dog, bred in Tibetan monasteries, are obscure. Well-known in India, the breed didn't become established in England until after World War II, but there are now about a thousand registered. This small dog (9 to 16 pounds, 9½ to 11 inches tall, with the smaller dogs being most highly prized), has proven to be a bouncy, alert pet. Its silky coat is long, its ears feathered, and its pride is a mane on neck and shóulders. Dogs can be black, black and tan, golden parti-colored, sandy, or white. (Utility: 2)

TIBETAN TERRIER: Said to have originated in the Lost Valley of Tibet, a region so remote that one

Tibetan Terrier

of these dogs was often given to infrequent visitors to make sure they got safely out of the country, this dog looks like a miniature Old English Sheepdog and is not a true Terrier. At home in Tibet it is an invaluable herder since its small size (14 to 16 inches at the shoulder, and weighing from 15 to 30 pounds) enables it to round up lost animals in mountain terrain inaccessable to larger dogs. In the Western world these dogs have made their way as excellent house pets. In the United States their profuse coats can be white, cream, gray, black, or golden. The English standard allows any color but chocolate. (M: 1; Utility: 2)

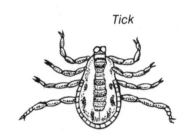

Tick

TICK: a parasitic insect (Acaridae) that can transmit tularemia (rabbit fever), Rocky Mountain spotted fever, canine babesiasis (malignant jaundice) and Q fever (*Coxiella burnetii*). Ticks mate while attached to their animal or human host and depend on the host's blood for survival. The engorged female, often the size of a large green pea, drops off and deposits two thousand or more eggs that in the larva state return to another human or animal and feed until satiated before falling to the ground. The same process is repeated in the nymph stage and again as adult insects. During these stages ticks can survive for many months without food.

Ticks can be found in the remote areas of a dog's body—in the ears, under the tail, or wherever the animal's fur is thickest. Care should be exercised in removing them. Use a tweezers, gloves, or piece of tissue. Try to remove the complete tick, for if the mouth breaks off and remains imbedded in the skin, sores can develop. It is hard to crush ticks, they should be burned or dropped in a jar of kerosene. If a dog is badly infested, the entire body, except for the head, should be immersed in a dip. There are sprays, powders, internal medications, and collars available for protection, but no one of these is infallible. If one's home or kennel is infested, seek advice from a veterinarian or exterminating agency.

TICKED: having isolated, small areas of black or colored hairs on a white coat.

TONGUE: the sound—barking or baying—Hounds make when they are on the trail of game.

TOURNIQUET: a tight band used to constrict the blood vessels and prevent excessive bleeding from a wound on the legs until professional help can be obtained. In an emergency it can be made from a handkerchief or tie, twisted taut with a spoon or stick. A tourniquet should always be applied between the wound and heart—i.e , above the wound. It should be loosened every ten to fifteen minutes in order to maintain blood circulation and prevent gangrene and then, after a short interval, tightened again.

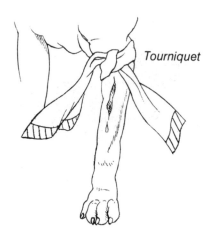

Tourniquet

TOXOPLASMOSIS: an infection caused by a one-celled germ (*Toxoplasma gondii*). The organism has been found in almost all mammals in most parts of the world. It usually causes no symptoms or discomfort, but occasionally it can lead to pneumonia or disease of the brain and eyes. Despite much research and many theories advanced about it, the exact life history and mode of transmission of the toxoplasma is still unknown.

TOY MANCHESTER TERRIER: see *Manchester Toy Terrier*.

TRACE: a dark stripe down the back of a Pug.

TRACKING: While all dogs possess an innate ability to follow a scent, training is needed to teach the animal to concentrate, persevere, and follow one particular trail to the exclusion of all others. Thus, to achieve a tracking degree, the dog must be presented with a set of increasingly complex problems to be mastered. In an AKC tracking test, for example, the dog must follow the scent left by a stranger for a quarter of a mile and end up by indicating or retrieving an article dropped at the end of a trail by the person it was tracking.

TRAIL: to follow an animal's scent.

TRAINING: see *obedience training, behavior patterns, bad manners*.

TRAVELING: Most dogs, since they are people-oriented, enjoy traveling in a car with their human family and present no problems. Your veterinarian can advise a remedy if your dog gets car sick. If you are going on an extended trip and planning to stay at hotels and motels, be aware that many do not allow pets in rooms. Check before you leave home.

If traveling within the boundaries of one country, dogs can travel by air or by train, whether or not their owners are going on the same carrier. Check with the specific airline or the railroad serving your dog's destination several weeks before you plan to ship it. Find out whether you must provide your own shipping crate and what its maximum size can be, or whether the shipper will provide the crate; inquire about what immunizations the dog must have had and what written form the carrier needs to assure compliance with its regulations; and ascertain how much in advance of scheduled departure time the dog must be at airport or station. On most airlines, dogs travel in relative comfort in pressurized, temperature-controlled compartments and in reasonable quarters on trains that will accept them for shipment.

If dogs are being shipped from one country to another by car,

plane, train, or ship, arrangements restrictions on the entry of dogs from other lands thoroughly explored. Many countries impose a lengthy (and expensive) quarantine on incoming dogs. You may find it more economical and no less hard on your dog to board it at a kennel near your home than to travel with it outside the country in which you live, particularly if you are not moving your residence permanently.

TRIALS: see *field trials*.

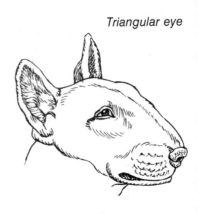

Triangular eye

TRIANGULAR EYE: an eye that is literally three-cornered since it is set in surrounding tissue shaped like a triangle.

TRICOLOR: having three coat colors—usually black, tan, and white.

TRICKS: The most important "tricks" that a dog should be taught are those that protect his life and make him a better citizen and home companion. As outlined in the entries on obedience training, these are (in no particular order):

to come when called
to know his place

to drop on command

to stay, sitting or standing, when told to

to heel

not to jump on people or furniture, unless so ordered.

Once a dog has completed intermediate courses in obedience training (see page 162), it is relatively simple to teach him tricks that will amuse or entertain one's family or visitors. A few of these are:

SHAKE HANDS: 1. The trainer has tapped the dog behind the right leg to make her raise the paw, at the same time giving the Command: "Pamela—shake hands!" At the fifth command Pamela is beginning to understand what's required. 2. That's the right idea, Pamela, but the wrong hand. 3. There we are. It took just 15 minutes to teach the two-year-old Golden Retriever this trick.

1.

2.

3.

To teach the sit-up: (a) place the dog in a corner, with his back close to the wall; (b) take both paws in your left hand and raise them so he is balanced on his haunches; (c) supporting him by his paws, give the command: "Sit Up!"; (d) repeat the command and with your right hand hold a tidbit beyond his reach, just above his nose; (e) after fifteen to twenty seconds, give him the reward and praise him; (f) repeat the exercise several times a day and in short order the dog will be supporting himself, away from the wall and from your guiding hand.

CARRYING AN OBJECT: Some dogs fetch and carry the owner's slippers or newspaper but Prudence enjoys answering phone calls and bringing the receiver to her owner. To teach a dog to carry: (a) place an object—a wooden

SIT UP: An exercise for small dogs, Tuffy enjoys this because she knows it will bring a reward.

dumbbell of the type used in obedience training is recommended—in the dog's mouth, giving the command: Take it!", (b) with your hand gently hold the jaws closed around the object; (c) after ten or fifteen seconds give the command "Out!" and remove the dumbbell or whatever the dog is carrying; (d) if he refuses to let go, repeat the command and take it away from him forcibly.

Once a dog takes an object and lets go of it willingly, give the "Take it!" followed by the first command taught in obedience training: "Heel!" Soon the dog will be trotting at your side carrying a basket, the daily mail, or whatever.

RETRIEVING: After a dog has learned to take an object and hold on to it: (a) with a long lead attached, throw something attractive, such as a tennis ball, a few feet from you and give the command "Fetch!" followed by "Come!" when he picks it up. Upon his return give the command "Out!" and take it from him; (b) if he refuses to come a tug at the leash will speed his return; (c) gradually increase the distance; (e) after he is letter-perfect on lead try without it. If he runs off, catch him, say "Shame!" sternly and reattach the leash. Eventually he will get the idea.

JUMPING: With the dog on lead walk him over a low hurdle or hoop held close to the ground, giving the command "Jump!" or "Over!" An upward pressure on the leash will give him a notion of what is expected. Raise the height gradually until his hind legs must leave the ground to clear the obstruction. Since most dogs love to jump he

Tuffy is quite willing to climb the ladder on command but her reproachful look seems to say: "What in the world purpose does this caper serve?"

will soon be performing admirably off lead. Note of caution: high jumping with immature dogs or breeds afflicted with hip dysplasia (see entry) should not be attempted.

DIVING: (particularly for sporting dogs, most of whom love the water), *ROLLING OVER* and *WALKING ON THE HIND LEGS* are some of the other exercises that dogs seem to enjoy. On the other hand there are a number of anthropomorphic tricks in which dogs are taught to imitate human behavior, which are out of character and seem somehow beneath a dog's dignity.

(Right) Four obedience champions await the next command from their owners.

Tuffy gamely held on while the vehicle slid down a small incline but she obviously wasn't enjoying the experience.

TUCK-UP: the rise in the underbody immediately behind the ribs; characteristic of speedsters like the Greyhound and the Whippet.

Tulip ear

TULIP EAR: an ear carried straight up and curved forward slightly.

TUMOR: an abnormal mass of cells that grow at their own pace and are not regulated by the normal body controls. Tumors can occur in any organ of the body or on the skin. They may be benign (those that do not spread and usually do not recur after removal) or malignant (those that are cancerous and spread rapidly throughout the entire body). Dogs should be inspected periodically for signs of lumps (especially in the mammary glands of the bitch) and nonhealing ulcers. If such conditions are found, veterinary advice should be sought promptly so that proper treatment can be initiated before the condition becomes too advanced. Operations, particularly on elderly dogs who are not in pain, are not always the answer to a tumor.

UV

UMBILICAL CORD: a cord containing the blood vessels necessary to supply food and oxygen to the unborn puppy. At birth the bitch will usually cut the cord with her teeth and separate it from the placenta. It is not advisable for the owner to ligate (tie) the cord or treat it with antiseptics.

UNDERSHOT: having lower jaw teeth that overlap or stick out beyond the upper jaw teeth when the dog's mouth is closed.

UNITED KENNEL CLUB: After the AKC, the second largest body for the registration of dogs in the United States. The UKC, a privately owned organization, specializes in the registry of American Coonhounds, Staffordshire Terriers, Eskimo dogs, American Bull Terriers, and English Shepherds, a breed developed but not yet recognized in the U.S. The UKC also licenses field trials, principally for American Coonhounds.

VENT: the anal opening or the area immediately around it.

VETERINARIAN: In the English-speaking world, veterinarians must be licensed by an examining, board, following completion of courses at an accredited school, before they can treat pets or other domestic animals. Courses leading to veterinary degrees are given at many colleges and universities throughout the world. Professional ethics preclude advertising, and since veterinary medical societies do not evaluate their members, perhaps the best method of finding a veterinarian is to make inquiries from pet owners in the area where one lives.

VITAMINS: chemicals that are present in very small quantities in natural foods and are essential for the proper growth and nutrition of the body. Vitamins A and D are needed for bone development in puppies, but if given in excessive doses are capable of causing bone disease. Vitamin B complex is important at all ages, but especially in older dogs. It can be obtained in capsules or in natural forms such as wheat-germ meal or brewer's yeast. Vitamin K is essential for normal blood clotting, and Vitamin E is thought to be associated with fat metabolism and fertility. A veterinarian should be consulted on the role played by vitamins in a diet.

Vizsla

VIZSLA: Also known as the Hungarian Pointer, or in England as the Hungarian Vizsla, this dog is an ancient sporting breed thought to have accompanied the Magyars when they invaded Hungary early in the tenth century. It would appear from early stone carvings that the lithe, muscular, medium-sized dog of today has changed very little over the intervening centuries. Lightly built (height 21 to 24 inches at the shoulder; weight, 40 to 60 pounds) with a docked tail, it is a stylish dog with a short, smooth, shimmering, rusty-gold colored coat. Various shades of dark, sandy yellow are permitted, but dark brown and pale yellow are undesirable.

Conditioned to hunt in wide expanses of flat, grain-growing land with very little cover to conceal dog or hunter, the Vizsla is a clever bird dog with a superior nose, which works with speed and caution where needed. It is an adept retriever and can handle waterfowl as well as the upland game for which it is most commonly used. In the home it is an energetic, affectionate companion. (Sporting: 1–3; Gundog: 2–4)

VOMITING: A symptom of many diseases, vomiting may be due to a virus, parasites, poisoning, peritonitis, brain injury, and many other conditions. Some puppies will vomit occasionally after eating grass or other objects. However, if the vomiting is frequent or continues for more than one day, the dog should be taken to a veterinarian for proper diagnosis and treatment.

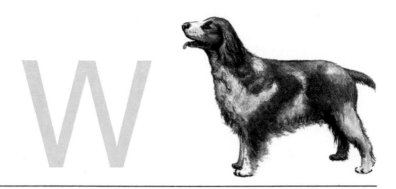

W

WAR DOGS: Dogs have been engaged in military pursuits since records of wars have been kept. In times past they were not only trained to attack other dogs but also wore spiked collars that enabled them to inflict serious injury on men and horses. In early

Dogs were trained to attack in mankind's first civilizations. In this Greek vase-painting (approximately 500 B. C.) two typical war dogs are shown aiding Hercules in the capture of Cerberus (British Museum, London)

times the Gauls sent dogs clad in armor onto the battlefield. In more recent wars German Shepherds, Dobermans, various working and Arctic breeds, and crossbreeds have been used in a more sophisticated fashion as messengers and sentries, on reconnaissance patrols, as pack animals and sled pullers, and to search for and lead rescue teams to wounded soldiers.

WART (papilloma): a hard, horny, painless growth of the skin. Warts are very common in older dogs, cause very little discomfort, and usually do not recur after surgical removal. One form of wart is due to a virus. It appears as a cauliflowerlike lump on the tongue, mouth, or lips, and is most often seen in dogs under one year of age.

WEANING: The process of weaning begins when puppies are three weeks of age and is completed by six weeks.

At three weeks, two parts evaporated milk and one part boiled water can be fed from a flat pie plate or saucer. Add an increased quantity of baby cereal to the milk each day.

At four weeks, feed the puppies the above milk and cereal formula four to six times daily, together with finely scraped meat or cooked eggs and a suitable calcium supplement.

Officers, men and dogs of His Majesty George V's armed forces during World War I, somewhere in northern France.

The American army trained German Shepherds, Bloodhounds and Doberman Pinschers for service in Vietnam. Here an attack dog lunges at an enemy during a practice session.

At five weeks, feed the puppies four times daily, but allow them to nurse the bitch at night.

At six weeks, the puppies should be completely weaned.

During the weaning period puppies should be handled frequently so they learn to trust and adjust to people. Exposure to noises, music, and traffic sounds should be started while the pups are still with their mother. This will reduce fear biting and enable each puppy to develop a people-oriented personality and adjust easily to its new home and to all the complications of our modern technological way of life.

During the weaning and post-weaning weeks puppies learn to play with each other and to socialize with other dogs. For this reason they should remain with their litter mates until at least seven weeks of age.

WEAVING: crossing of forefeet or hind feet, one over the other, when the dog is in motion.

WEIMARANER: Emerging from almost total obscurity within the past half-century, these gray all-purpose hunting dogs have captivated breeders in many parts of the world. They are natives of Weimar, Germany, and equally

Weimaraner

adept on land and in water. Once known as the Weimar Pointer, the animals are renowned for their good nose, bravery and speed. At one time they were the exclusive property of the Weimaraner Club and were difficult to acquire in Germany and virtually impossible to purchase elsewhere. Not until 1929, when an American was made a member of the club and allowed to bring back two of the dogs, was the breed seen in the United States.

Weimaraners are stylish in the show ring and excel in obedience competition. They make fine pets but, like many other breeds of gundog, prefer an outdoor life and the excitement of the hunt.

Weimaraner family with widely diverging points of view.

Standards call for a short, mouse-gray to silver-gray coat with a spot of white permitted only on the chest. In the United States dogs are from 23 to 27 inches tall; in England 22 to 25 inches. Weight ranges widely, from 55 to 85 pounds. (Sporting: 1–3; Gundog: 2–4)

WELSH CORGI: see *Cardigan* and *Pembroke Welsh Corgi.*

Welsh Springer Spaniel

WELSH SPRINGER SPANIEL: On land or water this dog, with its flat, silky, dark red and white coat, is a rewarding gundog for any kind of game. Unchanged in its present conformation for many decades in Wales and western England, the medium-sized dog (weight, 35 to 45 pounds) will, if trained as early as possible, make a steady, hard-working hunting companion. It is an instinctive and compulsive hunter and, untrained, will go off by itself in pursuit of game, forming habits difficult for the owner to break. Quieter than its English Springer Spaniel cousin, which it closely resembles, it is an affectionate, glamorous and docile household pet. (Sporting: 1–3; 2–4)

Welsh Terrier

WELSH TERRIER: A dog that has been called by many names over the years—including Old English Terrier and Black-and-Tan Wire-Haired Terrier—the Welsh Terrier continues to be the same dog it was more than a hundred years ago in Wales. It was bred for hunting badger, fox, and otter and has every bit of the courage needed for such pursuits, but is nonetheless an exceptional house pet, particularly for the young and agile who can keep pace with its bouncy activities. It is small (about 15 inches high and weighing about 20 pounds), sheds very little of its wiry black and tan or black grizzle and tan coat, and is a smart, playful companion and an alert watch dog. (Terrier: 1–2–3–4)

WEST HIGHLAND WHITE TERRIER: The exact origin of this small, perky, all-white Terrier is not known, but it is assumed that the dog is the result of breedings of the unwanted pure-white offspring of the Highland breeds. In time, the white terriers were selectively bred for color and type, and a distinct strain was developed.

Though bred as a hardy working Terrier, the Westie, which measures 10 to 11 inches at the withers, enjoys great popularity as a

West Highland White Terrier

lighthearted, independent family pet, a spunky watch dog, and a confident, crowd-pleasing show dog. Its characteristic Terrier coat of straight, hard outer hairs and soft undercoat requires little trimming. Long hair is left on the head to frame the face, giving emphasis to the desired Westie expression. Ears are small, pointed, stiffly erect, and never cropped. The animation of this charming dog is made clearly evident by the ecstatic quiver of its upright, short, but never docked tail. (Terrier: 1–2–3–4)

WESTMINSTER DOG SHOW: the most important event for owners and handlers showing dogs in the United States, and what Cruft's Show is to England. The first show was held in 1877, and was named after the Westminster Club, a sportsmen's group that had its headquarters in the Westminster

Mob scene at Westminster. Judge (center, back to camera) is testing the alertness of a Golden Retriever.

Hotel in New York and established a boarding and training kennel for the members' hunting dogs. The show has been held every year since 1877, generally at whatever Madison Square Garden was then serving New York City as headquarters for sporting events. The present Garden is somewhat smaller than its predecessors, so entries at this February event are limited to three thousand dogs. Three groups are benched and judged on one day and the other three on the following day.

WHEATEN: a pale fawn or yellow color.

WHEEL BACK: see *roach back*.

WHELPING: Birth or delivery of puppies is a complicated process. Whelping usually occurs from sixty to sixty-five days after breeding, but normal litters have been delivered at any time between fifty-six and seventy days after mating. Most bitches will deliver normally and without help if certain precautions are taken. The bitch should always be introduced to her box at least one week before the expected date of whelping. She should be kept in quiet, familiar surroundings and checked frequently by the owner. During the actual delivery, owners should stay close to the whelping box and be available to watch for complications. However, the owner should not interfere with the bitch or puppies without definite instructions from a veterinarian.

Signs of imminent whelping vary greatly. Usually the rectal temperature falls to 100 degrees or below, and the bitch will be restless, puff and pant intermittently, and start to dig up a bed in her whelping box. She may or may not refuse food. At this time the puppies drop into the lower portion of the abdomen, so that the bitch's flanks will appear thin and be soft to the touch.

These signs are followed by increasingly frequent straining efforts until the first puppy is born. If a bitch strains hard for one hour without delivering a puppy, a veterinarian should be consulted promptly.

Each puppy is preceded by a water bag and is enclosed in its own sack of fetal membranes. The placenta (afterbirth) is delivered with the puppy or very shortly afterward. Normally a bitch will open the sack with her teeth, lick the

Whelping box

233

puppy all over, and then eat the membranes and afterbirth and push the puppy onto her nipple. If she fails to open the sack, the owner should nick the membrane with a finger and gently rub the puppy's face with a towel until breathing starts. Under no circumstances should the owner pull on the umbilical cord or attempt to deliver the afterbirth.

Most bitches will deliver one or more puppies and then rest for an hour or more before resuming labor. During this rest period the owner may offer her a little water or milk. After the last puppy has been born, the mother will relax and settle down to nurse the litter. At this time she will appreciate a light meal of milk, eggs, and cereal and may be taken out to relieve herself.

For several days after whelping, a bitch may have diarrhea accompanied by a blood-stained discharge from the vagina, which may persist for a week or more.

WHIPPET: This small sight hound was developed in the 1830's by British miners who crossed small Greyhounds with Terriers to obtain a small racing animal that could provide the thrills of a racing sport in a limited area. Later crosses with the Italian Greyhound resulted in

Whippet

further refinement of the breed. There is little evidence of Terrier ancestors in the sleek, graceful Whippet of today, which has been known to attain a speed of 35 miles per hour over the standard 200-yard racecourse. Overshadowed by Greyhound racing, Whippet racing remains an amateur sport.

Strict size requirements in the American breed standard specify a height of 19 to 22 inches at the shoulder for males and 18 to 21 inches for bitches. Dogs measuring a half inch above or below the stated height limits are disqualified in the show ring. The English standard calls for a smaller dog, measuring 17½ to 18½ inches at the shoulder. Its short, smooth coat, like that of the Greyhound, may be any color.

Not only is the Whippet renowned as a racer, but it is currently popular as an elegant show dog and an intelligent, dignified house pet. (Hound: 1–2–3–4)

WHIPWORM (Trichuris vulpis): a small threadlike worm, found in the cecum and occasionally in the colon of the dog, which causes irritation and ulceration. Symptoms include periodic diarrhea that is often tinged with blood. Medical treatment is available and is usually effective, but stubborn cases may require surgical removal of the cecum to effect a permanent and certain cure.

WILD DOGS: In many parts of the world, generally living close to the habitations of man, exist packs of wild dogs. They range from the Dholes of Indonesia to the Cape Hunting Dogs of Africa, from the Buansnah of the Orient to the

This wild Dingo pup looks as though she could easily be domesticated.

Dingo of Australia. While some experts refer to all but the Dingo as "false dogs," the size, dentition, and family habits of these animals so closely resemble domestic animals as to warrant their inclusion as members of the dog family.

Except for the multi-colored Cape Hunting Dog all of these breeds are monochrome in shade, ranging from black to yellow or cream. All have prick ears set close to the sides of the head. Nearly all of them are trainable. Most of them live close to the homes of man, living off his garbage and retreating warily at his approach.

The Dingo, which most probably was imported to Australia by sail-ing ship centuries ago, is the only large non-marsupial on the continent. Generations ago it was domesticated and a family pet of aboriginal tribesmen who probably used the dog to flush game and bring it into the open. Today, except in remote outposts where the vanishing tribes live, it has reverted to the wild state and hunts sheep singly or in pairs.

Because of its taste for sheep-killing the Dingo is a highly unpopular animal and high bounties are paid for each killer dog exterminated. Nonetheless, despite annual massacres of Dingos and high fences which stretch for miles around sheep ranges, Dingos continue to flourish.

Cape Hunting Dog

The Cape Hunting Dog is another interesting wild or "false" dog. It has enormous rounded ears, only four toes front and back and no dewclaws, and a thin, fragile looking body atop long spindly legs. Its appearance is deceptive for the dogs, attacking in packs, are savage killers and more than a match for a lion.

WIRE-HAIRED POINTING GRIFFON: See *Pointing Wire-Haired Griffon*.

WITHERS: the highest point of the shoulders, behind the neck.

WORKING TRIALS: The Fédération Cynologique Internationale (FCI) awards international working-trial championships after two certificates have been won in two separate countries plus one first, second, or third prize. Dogs under fifteen months of age must meet additional standards. Most of these trials feature guard and protection dogs. (See also *Schutzhund*.)

Working trials are also held frequently in the United Kingdom and, to a lesser extent, in the United States, for Bloodhounds, wherein the dogs follow a stranger's scent. Dogs work either on a tracking leash or free, and are accompanied by one person (an owner usually) on foot. Judges equipped with maps follow on horseback to make sure the hound is not taking any short cuts. The trial ends when the Bloodhound correctly identifies the person it is tracking and places both forefeet on his shoulders. (See also *tracking*.)

X

XOLOIZCINTLE: Pronounced sho-lo-ees-quin-tlay, these hairless dogs nearly reached a point of extinction several decades ago but are now making something of a comeback. The species is perhaps the oldest in the Western Hemisphere and is not directly related to the Mexican Hairless. The dog is usually bronze, grey or grey-black with pink or brown patches permitted. The Xoloizcin-tle, sometimes spelled with an 'l' at the end, is recognized by the Mexican Kennel Club and the FCI.

X RAY: a special light ray that can pass through opaque parts of the body and produce a photograph. X rays are used by veterinarians to locate fractures of the bones and to examine fully many of the internal organs of the body. They can sometimes be helpful in the treatment of certain types of tumors.

Xoloizcintles watching the passing parade in Mexico City

Y Z

YORKSHIRE TERRIER: A tremendously popular Toy Terrier with a glamorous, long, straight, silky coat, this dog is now exclusively a charming house pet and a bright little show dog, whose weight must not exceed seven pounds. The Yorkshire probably developed from crosses of the Skye Terrier, which Scottish weavers brought with them when they moved into Lancashire and Yorkshire around 1850. The early Yorkshire Terrier was a bold rodent killer, but through selective breeding, the size of the dog has been greatly reduced and the length of its coat has been dramatically increased, making it no longer suited for its original duties. Unperturbed, the dog has adjusted well to a pampered existence and still retains the confidence and air of self-importance that is typical of the Terrier breeds.

Yorkshire Terrier

Puppies of this breed are born black and as they mature, a dark steel-blue color develops, extending over the body from the back of the neck to the root of the tail. Head, ears, chest, and part of the legs become a rich tan. The coat, parted down the length of the dog, may reach ground length and requires careful daily grooming. (Toy: 1–2–3–4)

ZYGOMA: the cheekbone of a dog. The surrounding muscles govern chewing and changes of expression around the dog's mouth.

BIBLIOGRAPHY

Note: Most of the books on the list that follows have been published on both sides of the Atlantic. Those that are especially recommended are starred.

General and Historical

*American Kennel Club. *The Complete Dog Book*. Revised, 1972.

Ash, Edward Cecil. *The New Book of the Dog*. 1938.

Baker, Charlotte. *ABC of Dog Care for Young Owners*. 1959.

Cross, Jeanette W., and Blanche Saunders. *The Standard Book of Dog Care*. 1952.

*Dangerfield, Stanley, and Elsworth Howell. *The International Encyclopedia of the Dog*. 1971.

*Hamilton, Fereleth. *The World Encyclopedia of Dogs*. 1971.

Hubbard, Clifford L. *Dogs in Britian*. 1948.

*Johnson, Norman H. *Complete Puppy and Dog Book*. 1965.

Jones, Arthur Frederick and John Rendel. *The Treasury of Dogs*. 1964.

*Kinney, James R. and Ann Honeycutt. *How To Raise A Dog*. 1946.

*Mery, Fernand. *The Life, History and Magic of the Dog*. 1968.

National Geographic Society. *The National Geographic Book of Dogs*. 1958.

*Vesey-Fitzgerald. Brian S. *The Book of the Dog*. 1948.

Woodhouse, Barbara. *The Book of Show Dogs*. 1959.

Somewhat More Specialized

Beamish, Huldine V. *Your Puppy and How to Train Him*. 1957.

Fox, Michael W. *Understanding Your Dog,* 1972.

Harmar, Hilary. *Dogs and How to Breed Them,* 1968.

Jones, Arthur Frederick. *Care and Training of Dogs*. 1949.

Koehler, W.R. *The Koehler Method of Dog Training*. 1962.

Nichols, Virginia Tuck. *How To Show Your Own Dog*. 1969.

Pearsall, Milo and Charles G. Leedham. *Dog Obedience Training*. 1959.

Pfaffenberger, Clarence J. *The New Knowledge of Dog Behavior*. 1963.

Saunders, Blanche. *The Complete Book of Dog Obedience*. 1954.

PHOTO CREDITS: *Lt. R. C. Ballard* p. 43. *The Bettmann Archive Inc.* p. 80 (bot.); p. 82 (bot.); p. 84; p. 126. *Bertel Bruun* p. 201. *Cardinali Studios* p. 181. *Culver Pictures Inc.* p. 79 (t.); p. 81 (bot.); p. 127; p. 190. *Walt Disney Productions* p. 84. *Harris Dunlap* p. 204; p. 205 (t. and bot.); p. 206 (t. and bot.). *Free-lance Photographers Guild Inc.* p. 12 Nellys; p. 13 J. Gajda (t.); p. 15 Ullmann (t.); p. 15 McLaughlin and Company (bot.); p. 16 Venture Photos by Herb Noseworthy (bot.); p. 30 E. M. Juedes, PSA; p. 34 J. Gajda (t. and bot.); p. 58 Ullmann; p. 62 Eugene Rosina; p. 78 Keystone; p. 87 J. Gajda; p. 88 J. Gajda (t.) and Gus Parras (bot.); p. 89 Peter Steiner (t. left) and J. Gajda (t. right and bot.); p. 100 Joyce R. Wilson (bot.); p. 109; p. 112 Keystone (t.); p. 125; p. 149 Ann Krausse; p. 173 J. Gajda; p. 182 Florence M. Harrison; p. 208 M. Warren Williams; p. 209; p. 230 Hal Mullin. *Giraudon* p. 227. *Keystone Press Agency, Inc.* p. 48; p. 54; p. 59; p. 65 (t. and bot.); p. 100 (t.); p. 110; p. 113; p. 114; p. 127; p. 130 Chris Ware; p. 144; p. 168 Chris Ware; p. 169; p. 189; p. 215; p. 229. *Kunsthistorisches Museum* p. 85 (t.). *Janis Leventhal* p. 7; p. 32 (bot.); p. 39; p. 101 (t.); p. 151; p. 152; p. 153; p. 154 (t. and bot.); p. 155; p. 156; p. 157 (t. and bot.); p. 158 (t. and bot.); p. 159 (t. and bot.); p. 160 (t. and bot.); p. 161 (t. and bot.); p. 162; p. 163 (t. and bot.); p. 164; p. 165 (t.); p. 192; p. 193 (t.); p. 221 (t. right); p. 222; p. 223 (t. and bot.). *The Metropolitan Museum of Art* p. 80–81; 82 (t.); 83; 84 (t.). *Nabisco, Inc. MILK BONE Brand Dog Biscuits* p. 52. *National Audubon Society* p. 13 Mary E. Browning (bot.); p. 17 Mary E. Browning; p. 31 Mary E. Browning; p. 33 Mary E. Browning (t.); p. 99 Max Hunn; p. 165 Joseph J. Shomon; p. 178 Mary E. Browning; p. 183 Mary E. Browning; p. 235 A.W. Ambler. *National Gallery, London* p. 85 (bot.). *New York Times* p. 55. *H. Armstrong Roberts* p. 14 (t. and bot.); p. 16 (t.); p. 29; p. 32 (t.); p. 33 (bot.); p. 101 (bot.); p. 121; p. 138; p. 146. *The Seeing Eye* p. 112. *John Tarlton* p. 93; p. 95. *United Press International* p. 52 (t.); p. 94; p. 131; p. 198; p. 200; p. 232; p. 237. *Herbert Wegner* p. 193 (bot.); p. 194.